ACROSS SUSSEX WITH BELLOC

In The Footsteps of 'The Four Men'

West Sussex County Council is pleased to be associated with this record of two walks by Bob Copper, one of the county's most well-known writers, following in the footsteps of Hilaire Belloc who spent much of his life in the county and who captured the spirit and identity of West Sussex in his work.

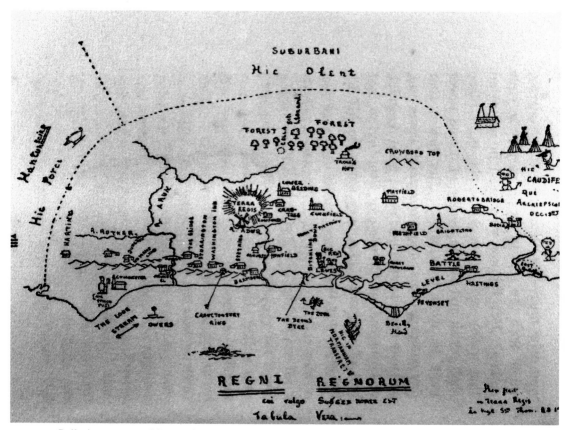

Belloc's own map of Sussex from The Four Men

ACROSS SUSSEX WITH BELLOC

In The Footsteps of 'The Four Men'

BOB COPPER

ALAN SUTTON PUBLISHING LIMITED

To Jon, Dot, Lucy and Tom

First published in the United Kingdom in 1994
Alan Sutton Publishing Limited
Phoenix Mill · Far Thrupp · Stroud · Gloucestershire
In Association with West Sussex County Council
County Hall · Chichester · West Sussex

First published in the United States of America in 1994
Alan Sutton Publishing Inc.
83 Washington Street · Dover · NH 03820

British Library Cataloguing in Publication Data

A catalogue record for this book is available from the British Library

ISBN 0–7509–0603–0

Library of Congress Cataloging in Publication Data applied for

Typeset in 11/12 Erhardt.
Typesetting and origination by
Alan Sutton Publishing Limited.
Printed in Great Britain by
The Bath Press, Bath, Avon.

Contents

Acknowledgements

The author would like to thank all those who in one way or another have contributed to the existence of this book: the inn-keepers who provided photographs of their inns; the people he met during the journey for their anecdotes and songs, their willing cooperation and hospitality; Charlie Eustace and the Peters, Fraser and Dunlop Group Ltd, for their kindness in granting permission to reprint Hilaire Belloc's copyright material; the West Sussex Library Services, and in particular Martin Hayes, principal librarian of local studies, for the selection, provision and permission to print the contemporary views of West Sussex; Brion Purdey, principal library manager of East Sussex Library Services and Brian Hart of Millgate Publishing Co. who performed similar services relating to early photographs of East Sussex; John Godfrey, Assistant County Secretary of West Sussex County Council; and finally Kim Leslie of West Sussex Record Office without whose enthusiasm, encouragement and practical support the book probably would not have seen the light of day.

Bob Copper

Introduction

I was nearing Heathfield and had been walking for three hours through steady, perpendicular rain, but I was dressed for the weather and well-shod, so my spirits were good and my feet were dry. So, also, was my throat, and my heart leapt when the sign of an inn appeared ahead of me as I rounded a bend in the road. I quickened my pace until I reached it, then stepped in through the door with the rain dripping off the end of my nose, and stood for a moment shedding pools of water onto the lino. The room was empty, apart from the landlord in his shirt sleeves leaning on the bar counter reading the morning paper. 'You look middlin' wet', he said, looking up with an unlit cigarette dangling from his lower lip and waggling precariously.

'I've just walked from Robertsbridge,' I replied.

'What's up, then,' he enquired with a wry grin, 'buses on strike?'

He was joking, of course, but I could see by his rather pitying look that he thought I was 'a few sheaves short of a load up top', as they say in these parts. The ordinary country dweller would look upon anyone who chose to walk ten miles across country, particularly in such weather, when other means of transport were available as being somewhat lacking in the essentials.

In spite of the recent renewed interest in country walking, there are still an astonishing number of people who look upon pedestrianism as a primitive and obsolete means of getting from one place to another, and never venture more than fifty yards from their motor cars. They do not know what they are missing. The physical and spiritual benefits of a long walk are almost incalculable – especially if you walk with a purpose. 'Thus, to walk without an object,' wrote Hilaire Belloc, 'is an intense burden, as it is to talk without an object. . . . On the other hand, walking with an object brings out all that there is in a man, just as talking with an object does.'

I was walking with a purpose and it was, in fact, Belloc who had put the idea into my head. I had first read his book *The Four Men* in 1939 and instantly fell under its spell. The very idea of four men walking through the leafy lanes and deserted byways of Sussex, from Robertsbridge in the east to South Harting in the west, was irresistibly appealing. They shared a passionate love of the county and as they walked discoursed freely on many diverse subjects; they argued; quoted, and indeed composed, poetry; sang outrageous songs; and behaved generally in an unrestrained and eccentric manner. They found inspiration in the beauties of the countryside and sustenance, in the shape of bacon, bread and beer, at wayside inns. They slept in little huts or houses to which Belloc fortuitously held the keys, and did all of those delightful, unconventional things that so many of us would love to do given the opportunity. I rose to the bait and knew I would not be content until I had done the walk myself.

It was a little over ten years before the chance to do so presented itself, and in 1950 I set out with a stout stick and a haversack to walk the route the original Four Men had taken.

It is well here, I think, to recall that three of the characters in the book – Grizzlebeard, an elderly philospher; the Sailor, a worldly man of the sea; and the Poet, an impecunious aesthete, who accompanied Myself, the narrator – are generally reckoned to be mythical figures who represented different aspects of the author himself. This theory is strengthened if we take a glance back into Belloc's life up to 1911, the year in which *The Four Men* was written.

Belloc was born in France in 1870 of an English mother and a French father, and at the age of six years, following the death of his father, he was brought to England where his mother had homes in London and Sussex. His love of the English countryside in general and Sussex in particular goes back to his boyhood days spent in the village of Slindon, West Sussex. Married in California in 1896, his American wife, Elodie, and he returned to England and had various homes in Oxford and London until they moved to Slindon in 1905. In the following year he bought King's Land at Shipley, near Horsham, West Sussex, a rambling house with five acres of land and a windmill, and there he spent the rest of his days until his death in 1953.

When Belloc wrote *The Four Men* he had already been Liberal Member of Parliament for South Salford from 1906 to 1910, and his earlier experiences at university had sown seeds of greatness in a very fertile and lively brain. He went up to Balliol College, Oxford, in 1893, where in the Oxford Union he made a deep impression as an orator of outstanding ability with radical and strongly held views on Church and State. He enjoyed remarkable academic success and, riding high in both literary and political circles, at one time seemed destined for the Bar. He narrowly and disappointingly failed to gain his Prize Fellowship at All Souls College. So, with a background like this it is easy to see how one of his self-appointed *alter egos*, Grizzlebeard, was a venerable philosophizing man of much worldly experience.

The sea always held a fascination for Belloc, and some of his best essays, in 'Hills and the Sea' for instance, are about sailing. He owned three boats over the years but his favourite was pretty certainly the *Nona*. She was a nine-ton cutter launched in 1870, like her owner, and was built for comfort and stability rather than speed, also, perhaps, likewise. A little over thirty feet in the keel, she was broad in the beam with a draught of about six feet and was frequently moored at either Littlehampton or Newhaven, from which Channel ports Belloc made many coastal and cross-channel voyages to Poole or farther round the coast, or over to Dieppe and other continental ports. He was never happier than when at sea and wrote lovingly about it in *The Cruise of the Nona*. At times like these Belloc was the ranting, roaring sailor man, singing sea-shanties and comic songs into the face of the wind as he stood at the helm with a bottle of wine in his hand. That is where the Sailor comes in.

Although he bore no physical resemblance to his description of the Poet there is no doubt whatsoever that he was equally, if not more, aesthetic than the pallid versifier who was encountered on the walk at Cade Street, near Heathfield. It is well known that he expressed a wish that he would be remembered as a poet rather than anything else, and I think it is true to say that his wish has been granted. He attained great heights of poetical expression in his prose alone, and we need look no farther than those haunting lines attributed to the Poet, when they spent the night in the little house at Ashurst, to be convinced that he was indeed a poet of great delicacy and distinction.

> The winter snow – the winter snow shall reverently fall
> On our beloved lands,
> As on Marana dead a winding sheet
> Was laid to hide the smallness of her hands,
> And her lips virginal:
> Her virginal white feet.

In Belloc we find the sagacity of the philosopher, the exuberance of the sailor and the tenderness of the poet, all encompassed in one rather bulky lump of clay. It amounted to something exceedingly close to genius.

However, had his companions been flesh and blood they could have walked abreast along most of the deserted country roads without anxiety at the time I first followed in their tracks. With the Second World War not long over and the restrictions on petrol still in force, motor vehicles were few and far between, the churches and inns were practically unchanged and a great deal of the scenery, too, was much the same as it had been when they passed by. The upheaval of war was over, the plodding peaceful rhythms of life had returned and the intense love of his homelands that Belloc conveyed so profoundly in his writings could be felt in the rural solitudes. Much, however, has happened since then.

Sussex is a county of great charm and diversity and – whether your preferences lie in rolling downland or fertile Weald; pine-clad heights or lonely marshes; white-walled cliffs on a lea shore or forgotten harbours and wooded creeks – you will find something to your taste within the county borders. Its undeniable beauty and appeal have been the inspiration of many prominent writers over the years and it must be among the most written-about counties in England. And that's how the trouble started, for therein were hidden the seeds of change – and change there most certainly has been.

In addition to the effects of the relentless expansion of the urban sprawl, the wide interest generated by the proliferation of works in praise of Sussex, in all their various forms, has led to a continuous invasion of sight-seeing visitors. And although the county has not suffered nearly so much as its neighbours in the south-west, it has had its full share of the tourist trade.

This, of course, is all very fine and desirable for the tourists and those who cater for their requirements, but what has happened to the places they visit? What has happened to the elfin world of Kipling's *Puck of Pook's Hill*? Where is the romance and drama of the smugglers' moonlight landings and the 'ponies trotting through the dark'? Where would you look to find Belloc's ancient and revered inns where 'the girls are plump and the ale runs brown' and the songs have 'a rousing chorus'? Where, in fact, will you find any part of that wonderful web of dreams spun by those who eulogized the county and which induced so many visitors to come here in the first place?

The consequent invasion has taken its toll and, sadly but incontravertibly, many of our most cherished heritages have suffered the fate of becoming tourist attractions. And you don't have to be madly misanthropic to recognize that the presence of people means pollution. When commercialism comes barging in through the front door, romance and beauty tiptoe hand-in-hand out at the back. Some of the most advantageous viewpoints on our Downs have been designated 'picnic areas', where, instead of the lonely shepherd and his flock, you will find crowded coach and car parks, overflowing litter bins and queues for the toilets. The air is loud, not with lark song but with the twitterings of transistor radios. The flagstones of the cathedral floor, too, are far more likely to be worn thin by the shuffling, neck-stretching curiosity of the multitudes than by the kneeling of the devout.

Atmosphere is a shy and subtle creature who dwells happily only where there is no fear of intrusion. Ironically, by coming in their thousands in search of cloistered silences and downland isolation, the visitors have unwittingly banished the very qualities they sought. On the face of things, then, Belloc's prophecy that the day would come when Sussex and the people in it would never more be what they were was remarkably accurate.

But, I wondered, while re-reading *The Four Men* recently, has that sad day really arrived or would it still be possible after all these years to cover the same ground, enjoy the same scenery and recapture, at least to some degree, the mood of Belloc and his companions in the days when the century was young? The cursory answer, of course, is no. But perhaps by avoiding the busiest roads and searching in forgotten corners one could find remnants of the peace and tranquillity of days gone by. Perhaps there are still to be found men and women of the old school living in remote areas and tucked away like pearls in the secret places of the oyster, in whose company one could still feel the pulse of the honest, earthy heart of Sussex.

I was seized with the idea of going over the route again in the footsteps of the Four Men, re-reading *the book* as I went. I chose to do it in the autumn to coincide as nearly as possible with the dates in *the book*.

Robertsbridge to Uckfield (19 miles)

As I walked up the steps and in through the door of The George at Robertsbridge the clock in the red-brick tower in the square struck five, and the venerable building opened its arms and clasped me to its bosom. Or so, at least, it seemed. How much of this was the result of the landlord's pleasant smile, the fond memories I had of a previous visit almost forty years before or the knowledge that I was following a distinguished precedent, it is difficult to determine. But as I climbed the crooked back stairs and followed my host along the narrow corridor to my room, I was pleasantly aware that those ancient floor boards had creaked to the tread of Belloc's boots, and the smoke from his pipe had helped to blacken the beams in the low ceiling overhead. For this is where he found himself on 29 October 1902, and where he made the heroic decision to forgo his worldly commitments and the world of business engagements, and go from this place to his home. To the 'steep bank over Stoke, the valley, the high ridge which hides a man from Arundel, and Arun turning and hurrying below. I smelt the tide'.

The fireplace at The George, Robertsbridge, where Belloc sat 'drinking that port of theirs and staring at the fire'

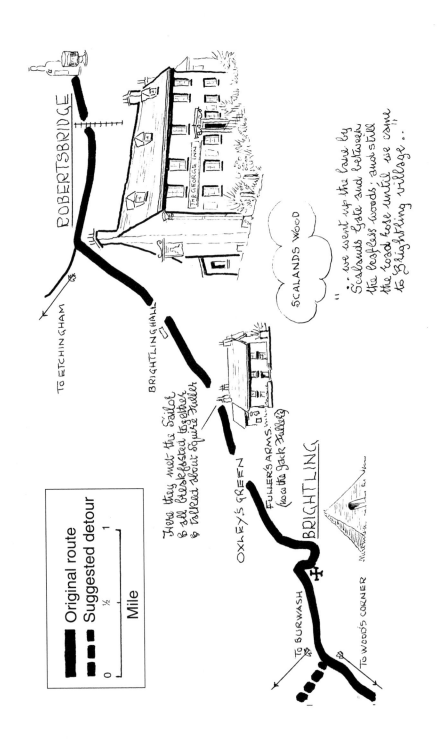

ROBERTSBRIDGE

TO ETCHINGHAM

THE GEORGE INN

SCALANDS WOOD

BRIGHTLING HALL

"... we went up the lane by Scalands Gate and between the leafless woods; and still the road tore until we came to Brightling village ..."

Here they met the Sailor & all breakfasted together & talked about Squire Fuller

OXLEY'S GREEN

FULLER'S ARMS. (now the Jack Fuller?)

BRIGHTLING

TO BURWASH

TO WOOD'S CORNER

Original route
Suggested detour

0   ½   1
Mile

Here it was, 'drinking that port of theirs and staring in the fire', that the idea of his epic walk across Sussex was born and which led, nine years later, to his writing the best-loved book of all of his prodigious literary output – *the book* whose itinerary I was about to retrace.

From the outside The George remains practically unchanged, but inside, on the ground floor at least, it has been developed beyond recognition. On my previous visit in 1950, as an act of homage to Belloc in gratitude for the immense amount of pleasure he has given so many of us in his writings, and also to fortify myself for the journey ahead, I had imbibed a dock-glass of port in front of the very same inglenook fire that had been his inspiration. But this was no longer possible. Instead of small, independent bars and parlours, practically the whole of the ground floor, including parts of what used to be the private quarters, has been opened out into one large saloon bar with a dining area. The fireplace has been blocked up and forms a backdrop to the bar, with a serried row of spirit optics ranged along the mantleshelf. However, these alterations have been carried out tastefully and there are still inglenooks and comfortable furnishings to preserve the friendly atmosphere of this historic inn.

Horace Walpole left a lively account of a somewhat hazardous journey in these parts in the eighteenth century, in the company of his friend John Chute, a Hampshire squire. Arriving here at about ten at night they determined to stop:

> but, alas, there was only one bed to be had: all the rest were inhabited by smugglers, whom the people of the house called mountebanks; and with one of whom the lady of the den told Mr Chute he might lie. We did not at all take to this society but, armed with links and lanthorns, set out again upon this impracticable journey.

On my arrival a group of young men occupied the far end of the long bar relaxing after a day's work. What did it matter that their car keys, cigarette packets and disposable lighters were plonked on the counter alongside their change from the previous round, replacing the clay pipes and chewing tobacco of earlier times? What matter if they drank pints of lager instead of pots of ale and they talked of cricket league placings rather than the recent landings of contraband goods at Pevensey Bay? It was a time-honoured scene and one that, in one form or another, must have been repeated under that roof on countless occasions, albeit not always quite so honourably.

One oddity in the room was the clock on the wall behind the bar, which must have been the product of later years. A narrow gilt frame surrounds its oval dial, which is the size and shape of the business end of a tennis racket. But the really singular feature about it is that the numerals appear as a mirror image of those on an ordinary clock and read anticlockwise, and the hands, including the secondhand, move in a corresponding direction. Confusing as this may sound it is remarkable how soon one becomes accustomed to this reversal of the norm, and I am sure the locals have become so familiar with its idiosyncracies that they are never in doubt as to whether or not it is time to head homewards or whether there is time for another drink before closing time.

On the wall is a framed photograph of Belloc taken in venerable old age, seated in slippered ease beside his own hearth with his favourite pipe in hand. Beside it is a notice telling of his visits to the inn and how some of the chapters of

The Four Men were written there. Also on display are the following stanzas from his poem 'The South Country':

> If I ever become a rich man,
> Or if ever I grow to be old,
> I will build a house with deep thatch
> To shelter me from the cold,
> And there shall the Sussex songs be sung
> And the story of Sussex told.
>
> I will hold my house in the high wood
> Within a walk of the sea,
> And the men that were boys when I was a boy
> Shall sit and drink with me.

After a splendid evening meal I was relaxing in the lounge when Ken, the landlord, came over and joined me in a post-prandial chat. He showed great interest in what I was doing, and over glasses of whisky we swapped favourite passages of prose and poetry from Belloc. He was reading from a book of quotations and I from *The Four Men*. Then I sang the songs from the book right there under the roof where it all began. The master looked down from his frame on the wall with what one likes to think was genial approval. We drank to his continuing existence, if not in this world then certainly in the next, and also in the hearts of those to whom he has given such joy and inspiration. His presence in The George that night was almost tangible.

Early the next day I crept out into the deserted street while the air was still calm and free of fumes. I turned eastward into Fair Lane up beside The Seven Stars Inn and past more delightful old houses. I followed the lane past Redlands Farm where the hop fields had just been cleared, and across the river valley to the north-east Salehurst church sat comfortably atop its wooded hill.

About half a mile farther on I came to the ruins of the Cistercian Abbey founded in 1176 by Robert de St Martin, who also built the bridge over the river, which gave Robertsbridge its name. Standing in the flat, fertile acres of the valley the remains of the abbey have been incorporated into a farmhouse, which itself is mellow with age, and some features of the original masonry are still visible from the outside. A considerable portion of the western gable is of the earlier structure, including a large, lancet window. The crypt, too, we are told, is in good preservation and opposite the house are two oast houses supported on walls of large stone with ancient foundations. There are also three or four free-standing stone ruins posing decorously in the well-tended gardens. I returned to the inn with an appetite adequate to accommodate the enormous English breakfast that was set before me.

Before setting out on the first stage of my journey I sat looking out of the window onto the square. I reflected that it was in this very spot that Belloc, who had thought himself alone, first became aware of the presence of Grizzlebeard, who had witnessed him thump the table with his hand in emphasis of his resolve to walk to his West Sussex homelands. And here they decided to join company and make the journey together.

'A man is more himself if he is one of a number,' Grizzlebeard had said, 'so let

The George Inn, Robertsbridge, where it all began

Remains of the chapel of Robertsbridge Abbey

us take the road together, and, as we go, gather what company we can find.' And after a night's rest they started off.

> Next morning, having slept profoundly, without giving a warning to anyone who had engaged us or whom we had engaged, by cutting ourselves quite apart from care and from the world, we set out with our faces westward, to reach at last the valley of the Arun and the things we know . . .

I checked my watch with the clock in the tower, which stood at eight-thirty, but they would not have seen that. It was built in 1920 to honour the local men killed during the Great War. Apart from this, the traffic and the contemporary dress of passers-by, the scene was much the same and it was not difficult to imagine the two of them as they set forth together – Belloc in his early thirties looking, most probably, very much as he does in the picture taken on his arrival in Rome (see jacket), just over a year before, on the completion of the pilgrimage that resulted in his book *The Path to Rome*. It is to be hoped, though, that he wore something more suitable for the chilly days of late autumn in England than the thin, linen suit 'that originally cost not ten shillings', and had been adequate for more southerly climes in high summer. It is safe to assume that he carried his 'great staff' and, perhaps, the 'small bag or pocket slung over my shoulder', which had accompanied him on his long continental journey and had contained when he started out 'a large piece of bread, half a pound of smoked ham, a sketch book, two Nationalist newspapers and a quart of the wine of Brulè'. I visualized him striding down the hill with his new companion, Grizzlebeard:

> a tall man and spare, well on in years, vigorous; his eyes were deep set in his head; they were full of travel and of sadness; his hair was the colour of steel; it was curled and plentiful, and on his chin was a strong, full beard, as grey and stiff as the hair of his head.

They were leaving behind them a small-town world of horsedrawn carriages and top hats; gas lighting and ankle-length skirts – a world that was to change so much, and heading out into the freedom of the open countryside, which has changed so little. It was just before nine when I set off to follow in their footsteps.

After passing the entrance to Gray Nicholl's factory, the home of those superlative bats with the red flash that have been wielded by the mighty men of cricket the world over wherever willow meets leather, the road westward out of Robertsbridge climbs steadily for about a mile and a half. The September air was warm but the sky was the colour of zinc and there was more than a suggestion of rain in the air. The trees were still in full, green foliage with few signs of the approaching autumn, and late summer flowers were blooming in the gardens.

Coming to a fork in the road I took the left-hand lane to Brightling and walked on with Scalands Wood on my left, presently passing Brightling Hall on the opposite side, while a fresh westerly wind brought a hint of the sea to mingle with the scent of the pines. Along this road the two of them had walked:

> up the lane by Scalands Gate and between the leafless woods; and still the road rose until we came to Brightling village, and there we thought that we would

High Street, Robertsbridge, early this century

step into the inn and breakfast, for we had walked four miles, and all that way up hill we had hardly said a word one to the other.

It was here with my pocket knife that I cut a stout, straight rod from a coppiced hazel to help me on my way, and it matched my footsteps for the remainder of the journey. It has accompanied me on many an expedition since that time, for a hand-staff is more than an aid to walking – it becomes a companion on the road and is a support in more than the physical sense. Izaac Walton tells us that the good Bishop of Salisbury, on seeing off a friend on his way on foot to Exeter, called him back and said, 'Richard, I sent for you back to lend you a horse, which hath carried me many a mile, and, I thank God, with much ease', and presently delivered into his hand a walking-staff, with which he professed he had travelled through many parts of Germany.

At Oxley's Green an isolated forge and blacksmith's shop lies back from the road on the right-hand side and, soon after, the sign of the inn situated at a crossroads tells us sustenance is at hand. It is the life-size figure of the gallant Jack Fuller himself, at one time squire of this parish, complete with top hat and umbrella, for this is the Fuller's Arms, now called Jack Fuller's, where Belloc and Grizzlebeard fell in with the Sailor:

Jack Fuller inn sign

But when we were come into the inn we found there a very jovial fellow with a sort of ready smile behind his face, and eyes that were direct and keen. But these eyes of his were veiled with the salt of the sea, and paler than the eyes of a landsman would have been; for by the swing of his body as he sat there, and the ease of his limbs, he was a sailor. So much was very clear. Moreover, he had a sailor's cap on with a shiny peak, and his clothes were of the sailor's cut, and his boots were not laced but were pulled on, and showed no divisions anywhere.

It was here that the three of them breakfasted together and here also, in 1950 when I first did the walk, that I enjoyed a thick gammon rasher of home-cured bacon and two eggs straight from the nest-box, and sat afterwards meditating on the goodness of life over a pint of bitter from the wood to aid digestion.

On that visit, my notes tell me, a brass ship's bell hung from a bracket on the outside wall beside the door to replace the ostler's bell. This is no longer there, but otherwise the exterior, including the stable buildings, are precisely the same – not forgetting the stone-built horse-mounting block close to the entrance, which is now seldom used.

The landlord greeted me at the door, a friendly man in a striped apron, which spoke of close association with the kitchen. The inn is well over half a mile outside Brightling itself and was opened here, converted from an old barn, by the redoubtable Fuller to replace the one in the village. The public life of The Green Man in the village street, it appears, was terminated by the advocates of abstinence and piety because its proximity to the church opposite seemed adversely to affect the size of the Sunday congregations. Not a very subtle approach, it could be said, to this age-old problem, and one is left wondering if this somewhat costly and clumsy attempt to load the dice against the devil actually worked.

I walked into the village where there were no visible signs of life. By this time the weather had thoroughly made up its mind what it wanted to do and I walked round the churchyard in steady, drenching rain. The dominant feature there is the large, twenty-five foot high stone pyramid, which is the last resting place of John Fuller (1757–1834). He was a country gentleman and the squire of Rose Hill, the county seat of his family, who made their fortune from the Sussex iron industry. Their coat of arms bears the legend *Carbone et Forcipibus* ('By Charcoal and Tongs'). He was a very colourful character – 'a large man who wore his hair behind in a pigtail', and fitted to a T the description of a typical county squire of those times given in a local booklet of Fuller by Geoff Hutchinson, 'a wealthy, bulky, beer and port drinking man, a jolly fellow, rough spoken, but with a heart of gold'.

While Member of Parliament for East Sussex, Fuller was conveyed on his regular visits to Westminster in a great coach drawn by six hefty shire horses, well provisioned for the hazards of the journey with coachmen and footmen armed with swords and pistols. He was renowned for his forthright and outspoken manner and, being called to order by the Speaker on one occasion, he stood his ground and roared, 'Do you think I care for you, you insignificant little man in the wig? Take that!!' Whereupon he snapped his fingers in the faces of them all. He was, however, seized upon and carried from the House by the Sergeant at Arms and his minions. During his political career he declined a peerage offered by William Pitt the Younger with: 'I was born Jack Fuller and Jack Fuller I'll die.'

There are many tales told of his eccentric behaviour. He was a benefactor to Brightling church, and, among other things, built the handsome oak-panelled choir gallery there. In 1820 he provided a barrel-organ to supplement the singing

Jack Fuller's tomb in Brightling churchyard

of the choir, the male members of which he decked out in white smocks, buckskin breeches and yellow stockings, while the ladies were provided with red cloaks. Being still dissatisfied with the overall tonal effects, he went to a music shop when he was next in London and asked advice of the proprietor. 'Try a trombone', came the suggestion. 'Send twelve!' was his imperious command as he turned and strode out of the door.

There are also a number of follies hereabouts that remain tangible evidence of Fuller's eccentricity or, more likely, his beneficence to the parishioners, for it is believed that some of his more extravagant enterprises were put in hand to provide work for the local men during winter. The wall round Brightling Park almost certainly was one of them.

Needless to say, numerous legends have grown up around the many follies of 'Mad Jack', as he was sometimes called, but sadly the richest and most colourful of them all has been exploded in the harsh glare of latter-day prying. It was held that he was interred within his pyramid mausoleum sitting at a table laid with a meal and a bottle of claret to hand, dressed for dinner, wearing a top hat and with broken glass strewn on the floor to keep the devil at bay. The tomb now stands open to the gaze of the inquisitive and the legend is exposed as a myth. There are certain people who love to go round trampling on other people's dreams and kicking down the sandcastles built by the romantics. I much preferred the fiction to the fact.

I walked round the pyramid while the rain pattered down on the leaves overhead. Otherwise all was still. The joints in the stonework were caulked with moss, and here and there a debilitated specimen of rosebay willow-herb found a precarious roothold. I had walked into the village and round the burial ground apparently unseen, and the mood of the place was undisturbed. I felt I was very close to the inner heart of things. The sombre green of the old yew trees, the ancient headstones and well-worn flagstone path bore silent witness to the past and, indeed, the spirit of Squire Fuller was still abroad.

I went into the church after shaking the rain from my hat in the porch. A marble bust of Fuller is on prominent display and beneath it the inscription, *'Utile nihil quod non honestum'* ('Nothing is of use which is not honest'). This would please him for that was the precept by which he liked to be known, and he warmed to the title 'Honest Jack Fuller' in preference to the names of a lighter vein, like that referring to his ample bodily proportions – 'Hippopotamus'.

Affixed to the north wall are plaques and tablets that tell a story that breathes the very essence of the long and leisurely manner in which events unfold in the life of remote villages such as this. John Batys, a one-time owner of Socknersh Manor, an estate with a noble and still handsome manor house about two miles north-east of the village, died in 1476, bequeathing to the church fourteen acres of land called Levettys. This fact was recorded on a brass plate and fixed to the interior wall of the church. Sometime later it was torn down and stolen and, as it was to all intents and purposes lost for ever, and in the absence of any evidence to prove otherwise, the church lost the ownership of the land and it was put to private use.

More than 150 years later someone found the brass plate broken in two pieces lying at the bottom of a deep well on the South Downs, at least twelve miles away, and in due course, through the Court of Chancery, the land was restored to the church and the recovered brass plate restored to its original position. In 1635 a further plate was added telling the whole sad story, which had ended so satisfactorily:

> whoe ever thov art who readest the Svperinscription know the good intention of the said Master John Batys was by some ill mynde deverted and the Lands called Levitts converted to private vse from this church for many yeres . . .

Brightling church with Jack Fuller's tomb

But all was put to rights in the High Court of Chancery

> . . . on the first day of Febvrary in the eleaventh yere of the reigne of ovr soveraigne Lord Kinge Charles Annoo Dni 1635 Ratyfyed and confirmed in all poynts.

Once out of the village a panoramic view opens out to the north and east across the valley of the river Dudwell, and about half a mile further on I found myself in something of a dilemma. The road forks right to Burwash and left to Dallington. The purist in me favoured the latter as this was the way Belloc must have gone, but, knowing that the road west from Wood's Corner to Three Cups Corner makes little provision for travellers on foot and motor traffic is fairly heavy, the pragmatist said no.

On my first walk I had stuck to the original route and at Wood's Corner had come out on the Heathfield road, which at that time was very quiet. I had also diverted and walked a couple of hundred yards east of the Swan Inn and taken a close look at the Sugar Loaf, a conical building some thirty feet high standing in a meadow with no obvious practical use. You can still visit it today. There is a door and several windows, all but one of which have been blocked up, and it is reputed to have been lived in by an old man who brought up his family there. It is also said that it was once the refuge of a hermit, but this must refer to a different incumbent and probably an earlier period. It would be quite impossible for one man to combine two such diverse roles, particularly within such a confined space.

Regardless of what has happened since the Sugar Loaf was built by Jack Fuller, it is one of his renowned follies and, according to one story, probably the most

The Sugar Loaf (one of Jack Fuller's follies), Brightling

frivolous and endearing. Having made a bet that he could see the spire of Dallington church from his home at Rose Hill, and then discovered that he was wrong, he caused this peculiar structure to be erected in one night in order to prove otherwise – at least to the satisfaction of the other party to the wager, who was due to visit the area the next day.

All of this notwithstanding, in view of the discomfort, not to say danger, of walking a busy country road with no footpaths, I took the road to Burwash. As I walked I mused on the reason why Belloc had looked upon Burwash with such disfavour. I took *the book* from my haversack and turned to where at the Fuller's Arms Grizzlebeard was holding forth in true Bellocian style in praise of the county of Sussex, declaring that:

> we were the first place to be created when the world was made, and we shall certainly be the last to remain, regal and at ease when all the rest is very miserably perishing on the day of Judgment by a horrible great rain of fire from Heaven. Which will fall, if I am not mistaken, upon the whole earth, and strike all round the edges of the county, consuming Tonbridge, and Appledore (but not Rye), and Horley, and Ockley, and Hazelmere, and very certainly Petersfield and Havant, and there shall be an especial woe for Hayling Island; but not one hair of the head of Sussex shall be singed, it has been so ordained from the beginning, and that in spite of Burwash and those who dwell therein.

Of all the places in Sussex, I wondered, why was Burwash the only one to rouse his ire? Could it possibly be that at that time a contemporary of his, a writer and poet of renown and also a lover of the county, lived there in a house called Bateman's and would have answered to the name of Rudyard Kipling? Perish the thought!

At the top of the hill I left the road and forked left onto a footpath. Close by stands Brightling Needle, another of Fuller's extravagances, which is a stone column 65 feet high, marking the highest point for many miles around at 197 metres above sea level. It is reckoned to have been erected to celebrate the Duke of Wellington's victory at Waterloo in 1815.

The weather had closed in and the rain was now accompanied by a thick mist, so I was denied the view that I knew existed to the south across the Pevensey Levels to the coast, some ten miles distant. Visibility was very limited and the successive ridges of wooded hills over which I looked faded, each with an additional touch of white from the celestial palette, until they melted into a blanket of grey.

I have frequently found when walking that the rhythm of my stride sets up a similar metre in my head, to which words can be strung in a form of simple verse. Unbidden the following lines came to mind:

> O, have you smelt the Sussex air
> In soft, September rain,
> When pheasants range the stubbles wide
> To lease the fallen grain?
>
> And have you climbed a glistening stile
> That wears the rain like jewels,

And lingered where the bracken bends
Round silent, rain-pocked pools?

O, have you trod the beech-mast ride
Beneath green dripping sprays,
And trudged the deep-hooved, puddled path
Of ancient bridle ways?

And has your heart been captured
By the timeless woodland mood,
That tells of pads and poachers
Since the days of Robin Hood.

At this point I reached Little Worge Farm, where a herd of matronly Friesians were being driven in by a boy on a tractor, their pendulous udders bulging with the milk that would be left on tomorrow morning's doorsteps in some distant town.

Following on in the same direction I passed through a thickly wooded area along seldom used pathways carpeted with beechmast and previous years' fallen leaves, and through ancient hollow ways between steep banks under a canopy of Spanish chestnuts and sapling hazels. Several large trees were lying prone with their saucer-shaped root systems standing vertical and exposed to the air, where they had fallen victim of the hurricane of 1987.

Presently the path dropped down to Glazier's Forge, where the Willingford stream trickles unconcernedly under an ancient stone bridge, threading its way over a stony bed in search of lower lands. Three hundred years ago the woodlands would have been clamorous with the racket of a waterwheel operating a forge hammer, and the bustle and shouting of the iron-workers, for this is the heart of the one-time Sussex iron industry. But this morning, in sylvan tranquility, the mellow tiled house built for the iron-master in about 1650 stood mutely in the rain dreaming of other days.

I strode on up the hill beyond, thinking of many things, one thought leading to another. When walking long distances alone with the body fully occupied in the mechanics of striding over the ground, the mind is released from compulsory employ and enabled to wander at will, exploring all of the little byways of thought that branch off in unpremeditated and entirely unpredictable directions. A combine harvester pulled out through a gap in the hedge ahead of me and made off down the lane, leaving behind a field of stubble drawn in long, straight lines like the bristles of a worn-out scrubbing brush. I could see by the spillages on the headlands that it was barley – good, golden maltster's grain – even at this moment, probably, heading for the malthouse, and from there, of course, to the brewer.

Autumn is a wonderful time of year – a period of ripeness, fruition and fulfillment – potato fields are cleared; orchards stand ready for the pickers; hopfields are stripped, leaving crooked poles and broken strings; oast houses are filled to capacity – O, the tantalizing aroma of hops; ripened blackberries hang in clusters in the laneside hedgerows; purple sloes and reddened hips and haws glisten in the rain. Drifting into my mind came a picture of the same scene on an

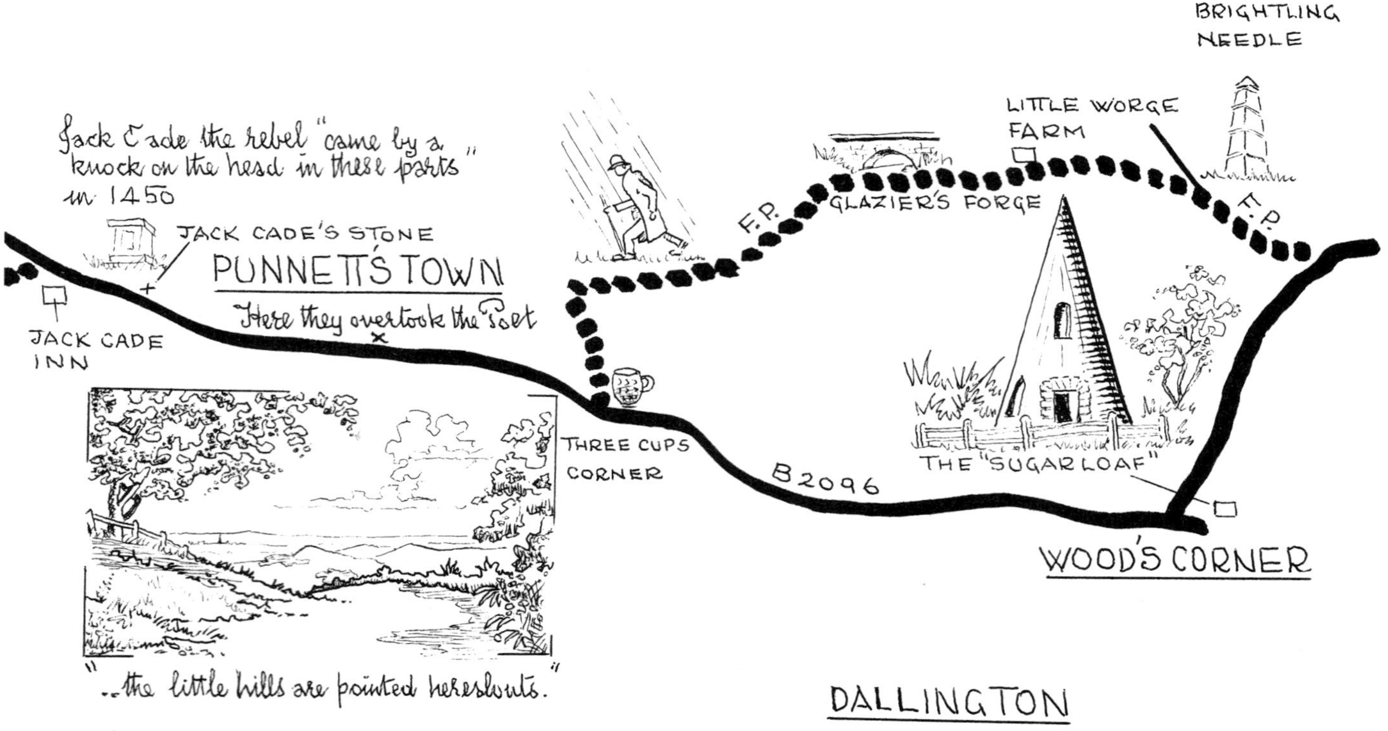

BRIGHTLING
NEEDLE

F.P.

LITTLE WORGE
FARM

F.P. GLAZIER'S FORGE

THE "SUGAR LOAF"

WOOD'S CORNER

B2096

THREE CUPS
CORNER

DALLINGTON

Jack Cade the rebel "came by a
knock on the head in these parts"
in 1450

JACK CADE'S STONE
PUNNETTS TOWN

Here they overtook the poet
X

JACK CADE
INN

"... the little hills are pointed hereabouts."

evening in June: the white innocence of bramble blossom; the pastel-pink of the dog rose; the scent of honeysuckle; the haunting sweetness of summer; long, light evenings; cricket on the green; the invasion of the village inn after the match; the post-event opinions of criticism or praise; the pint glasses of cool, bitter beer – limpid, amber and sparkling like the glint in a pheasant's eye.

Whoops! My feet almost went from under me as they slithered on the muddy path and I returned to the grey, sodden reality of the morning with a bump.

Out on the other side of Dallington Forest the rain eased off, and I turned south on to a path that led me down to Three Cups Corner on the Heathfield road, opposite the inn. Just down the lane that runs to the west is a notice on a gate: 'David Bysouth, Rushlake Green. Wooden Wheels, Shafts, and Horse-drawn Vehicles made and repaired. Wheelbarrows made to Order. Closed on Sundays.' And on a separate, reversible board, to indicate the opposite when the situation prevailed: 'Workshop Open'.

As I turned in through the gateway and crunched up the gravel path past David's bungalow, called, aptly enough, The Hub, I could see a group of four figures standing round a ring of fire burning fiercely in the middle of the yard. They must have heard my approach, but no one looked up – all of their attention was focused on the blaze before them. I sensed an air of mounting tension and it became obvious that an important stage in some kind of operation was rapidly approaching. I was puzzled as to what it was.

Three men stood evenly spaced around the circumference of the fire holding long iron bars of about five feet in length with an angled fork at the lower end. The fourth person, who turned out to be David's wife, was standing by with a watering can. At a given signal from David they went into action plunging the tyre-dogs, for such they were, into the glowing embers, and at a second signal they lifted out a red-hot wagon-wheel tyre of ¾ inch thick iron, four and a half inches wide and five feet in diameter. They carried it swiftly across to where a large wagon-wheel was placed in readiness at ground level on the tyring anvil, a flat, circular platform of heavy 1½ inch thick iron about six feet across, with a hole in the centre to accommodate the hub or nave.

With swift but unhurried expertise they lowered the tyre down on to the wheel, the outside rim of which David had renewed with curved oak segments called felloes. Immediately it burst into a coronet of small flames like a chandelier, at the same time sending up clouds of smoke, which floated upwards and melted into the overhanging greenery of an ash tree.

That was the signal for Mrs Bysouth to play her part. She poured the contents of the can around the rim, extinguishing the little conflagrations and creating volumes of steam, which mingled with the smoke and completely enveloped the four of them. There was a sizzling sound like a fish and chip shop on a Saturday night, and I could hear David coaxing the tyre down onto the wheel with a sledgehammer. As the steam cleared I could see the other three continually dousing the wheel rim with water while David continued to drive the tyre fully home, tapping first here and then there with the expert touch of a surgeon. At last the iron was fully shrunk onto the wheel, tying it in towards its centre until it was as tight as a drum and you could almost hear it ring when David tapped it. He later told me that that is why it is called a tyre – that is, tie-er. The whole operation had taken seven minutes and was carried out with the methodical assurance that comes only from years of experience coupled with an inherited knowledge of traditional skills.

'En't a lot in it, is there?' said one of them at last, eyeing it from various angles.

'No, I think she's jest about there,' replied David. 'Best look at t'other side, tho.' And the wheel was released from the anvil, lifted and turned with care, for the tyre was still very hot, and given a final examination. Then it was wheeled away and leant against a cart standing nearby to cool.

The job done, David looked up and acknowledged my presence. I told him how much I had enjoyed watching a scene that had been common enough sixty years ago. I had noticed that, though the day was very warm, they wore shirts or jerseys right up to their necks and down to their wrists, and he told me that that was to prevent scorching from the intense heat of the tyre when it is first taken from the fire.

In his workshop I looked around me while they peeled off their overalls. It was a scene of workmanlike efficiency. New wooden cartwheels of different sizes and in varying stages of completion stood leaning against the far wall near a stack of seasoned timber of the appropriate shape, size and grain to be fashioned into shafts, wheel spokes and floorboards when the necessity arose. Saws, calipers and set-squares hung from nails in the wall; chisels, gouges and spoke-shaves each in its respective niche in the tool rack; and even the planes and other tools in current use on the benchtop were only in mild disarray. There was an air of unfussy organization and, apart from the smell of woodsmoke, which had drifted in from outside, there was a pleasant aroma of linseed oil and the sour-beery smell of seasoned oak shavings, which littered the floor under the bench.

We all adjourned to the Three Cups and, there in the bar over glasses of beer, David told me how he had been brought up in the trade in Cambridgeshire and used to help in his father's forge and wheelwright's shop while he was still at school. He had been at Rushlake Green for ten years, Heathfield for twenty and Mayfield for six before that, and, acclimatized to Sussex and her ways as he must have become during that long time, like a true countryman he still holds a warm affection in his heart for his native county.

David described the old methods of working before the days of power tools, oxyacetyline cutters and electric welders – a job that called for strength, skill and sweat. It was pleasant to sit in the presence of a true craftsman – one whose trade is part of his life, whose tools are handled with affectionate care and whose finished handiwork is regarded with pride.

Through the window I could see that the rain had returned in no uncertain manner, and it took a determined effort of will to drag myself away from such pleasant company and the friendly fug of the bar. But I shouldered my pack, picked up my hazel and took to the road again. I was now back on the original route once more and my diversion had cost me nothing in terms of *the book*, for it was back at the Fuller's Arms that 'we all three set out under the high morning for Heathfield, and were ready to talk of Jack Cade (who very nearly did for the rich, but who unfortunately came by a knock on the head in these parts . . .)'.

And here I was, after passing through Punnett's Town, approaching Cade Street itself. It was here that they overtook the Poet:

and we saw that as he walked his long limbs seemed to have loose joints, his arms dangled rather than swang, he steered no very straight course along the road, and under his felt hat with its narrow brim there hung tawny hair much too long, and in no way vigorous. His shirt was soft, grey and dirty, and of wool, and his collar made one with it, the roll of which just peeped above his throat, and his coat was of velveteen, like a keeper's, but he was not like a keeper in any other way, and no one would have trusted him with a gun.

He was invited to join them by Grizzlebeard with: 'Only come westward with us and be our companion until we get to the place where the sun goes down, and discover what makes it so glorious.'

I was now little more than a mile from Heathfield and was walking on the north side of the road when I came to a large, square stone, erected to mark the spot where Jack Cade was apprehended. I stood and read the inscription while the rain dribbled from the brim of my hat:

Near this spot was slain the notorious rebel Jack Cade by Alexander Iden, Sheriff of Kent, A.D. 1450. His body was carried to London and his head fixed upon London Bridge. This is the success of all rebels and this fortune chanceth ever to traitors.

Jack Cade Stone

Soon after this I saw the sign of the Jack Cade Inn, which in Belloc's time was known as the Half Moon, although he makes no mention of it.

The Jack Cade Stone, Cade Street, near Heathfield

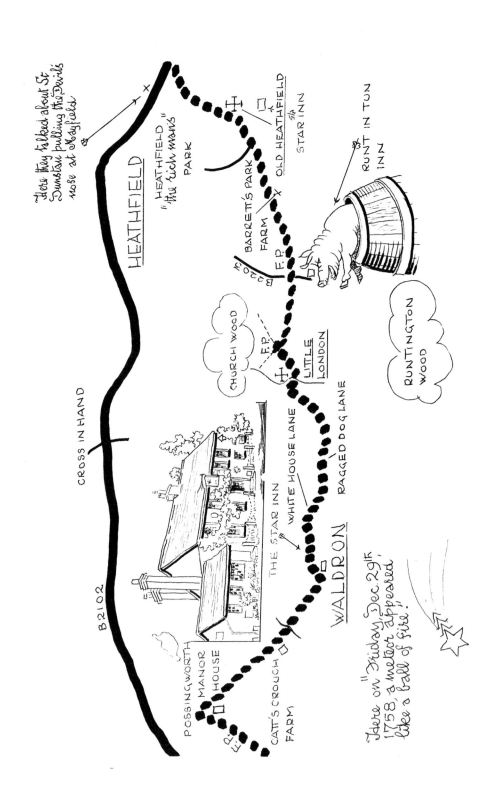

Here they talked about St Dunstan pulling the Devil's nose at Mayfield

HEATHFIELD

HEATHFIELD "the 'rich man's'" PARK

OLD HEATHFIELD STAR INN

BARRETT'S PARK FARM

F.P.

B2104

RUNT IN TON INN

CROSS IN HAND

CHURCH WOOD

F.P.

LITTLE LONDON

RUNTINGTON WOOD

B2102

WHITE HOUSE LANE

RAGGED DOG LANE

THE STAR INN

WALDRON

POSSINGWORTH MANOR HOUSE

CAT'S CROUCH FARM

Here on "Friday, Dec. 29th 1758, a meteor appeared like a ball of fire."

Belloc is unspecific as to how he and his friends travelled west from Heathfield, but just outside the village they paused, sat down, and considered their companionship joined and the first stage of their journey towards the west accomplished:

> So we sat down outside the village at the edge of a little copse which was part of a rich man's park, and we looked northward to the hill of Mayfield, where St Dunstan pulled the Devil by the nose; and they keep the tongs wherewith he did it in Mayfield to this day.

Then they discussed the matter: 'Well, as we sat there in Heathfield, we debated between ourselves by which way we should go westward, for all this part of The County is a Jumbled Land.'

It was finally decided 'that there was nothing for it but to go by the little lanes to Irkfield, particularly remembering The Black Boy where these little lanes began'. There is no such place as Irkfield, so here we must read Uckfield and wonder if the great man found the little town irksome.

It is most likely that the travellers kept to the main road as far as Blackboys, but this, as the A265, is far too busy nowadays to invite the seeker of romance. I, therefore, forked left at the pub down toward Old Heathfield, for it is fairly obvious that when Belloc wrote 'Now in those days Heathfield was a good place for men, and will be again', he was referring not to the newer part of the town, which was spawned by the arrival of the railway, but to the ancient part by the old church, which is referred to quite distinctly today as Old Heathfield, as if to make certain that no one will confuse it with its rather brash younger relative.

This morning Heathfield was dull, dripping and deserted. On the long approach to the church, with the rich man's park over to my right, I saw not

Mutton Hall Hill, Heathfield. 'Now in those days Heathfield was a good place for men, and will be again'

another human soul. The slender, shingled spire stood tall against the hodden grey of the sky and a dozen or so swallows, impervious to the rain, swirled around it like smuts from a chimney. Beneath it a double-gabled house with brick chimneys faced up the road towards me.

I entered the churchyard through the lych-gate and on the south of the church found the sturdy, stone-built Star Inn. This was originally constructed to house the workmen employed on the erection of the church and the walls are of the same honey-coloured stone. One or two old houses nearby, also of warm ashlar, look as if they might have been built from material left over when the church was completed, and appear to date from the same period.

On Reverend Robert Hunt, one time vicar of this parish, falls the distinction of having conducted the first ever Anglican Holy communion service on American soil. He sailed across the Atlantic and at Jamestown, Virginia, in 1617, administered the sacrament to a handful of settlers. In the church is a splendid stained-glass window commemorating this historic event, depicting Robert Hunt serving a group of communicants in Stuart-period costume, watched with curiosity by two Indians – a man in a feathered head-dress and a small child seated on the ground. It is an edifying thought that from this remote little village, as it must have been in those days, originated the tiny spark of faith that lit the torches that carried the flame of Protestantism throughout the length and breadth of the USA.

Here for a short distance I walked along by the high park wall, which, so they say, was built by one pair of hands in three years. Those hands certainly belonged to a competent and hardworking man, for the wall is three miles long.

I took a track down to Barrett's Farm and a little later passed north of White Chimneys Farm, where a couple of dogs dashed up to greet me, their wagging

The church and lych-gate at Old Heathfield

tails betraying the inferred ferocity of their barking. Half a mile farther on I came out onto the Horam to Heathfield road, close to the Runt-in-Tun Inn with its punning signboard of a pig (no doubt a runt) in a barrel (which must be a tun), and I knew then that I was at Runtington. Picking up the path slightly offset to the right, I continued up into the woodland, which is part of Runtington Wood, and where the path is bisected by another I turned half left onto it towards Little London. This brought me out by the little church there.

I took the lane opposite the church in a south-westerly direction past a school called the Spinney, and this took me into Ragged Dog Lane, which eventually meets Whitehouse Lane in a T-junction. I turned left and, after about half a mile, came to Waldron and The Star Inn. The feature of this pleasant village pub, which most captured my attention, was an old water-clock that was found in the cellar by a previous landlord, now restored and on display in the bar.

The colourful sign affixed to the wisteria-clad wall outside depicts the inn itself under a night sky and the heavenly presence of a radiant star. This may or may not be a reference to a happening hereabouts over two hundred years ago, which was faithfully recorded by Thomas Turner, a general-stores keeper and one time schoolmaster of East Hoathly, a small village some three miles to the south-west. He is one of the best-loved of the Sussex diarists and gives fascinating glimpses of life in these parts in the mid-eighteenth century:

On the even of Fryday, Dec 29, 1758, a meteor which appeared like a ball of fire falling from the clouds to the earth. It seemed as if it fell about Waldron leaving a trail of sparks behind it as it descended, its bigness was at last about the size of a large ball, tho' at first almost like a moon, and extremely light.

Then, with an admirable burst of honesty, he confessed, 'I imagine fear and surprise hath exaggerated many of the above circumstances.' Eighteen months earlier in May 1756 he had reported several explosions heard in the bowels of the earth like an earthquake in the parishes of Waldron and Hellingly.

According to his diaries Turner fought a constant and not entirely successful battle with the demon alcohol, and from time to time found himself 'a little matter enlivened with liquor but no wayes drunk', or 'contracted a slight impediment in my speech occasioned by the fumes of the liquor operating too furiously on my brain'. On 8 December 1759 we read:

we drank a great many loyal toasts. I came home after eleven after staying in Mr Porter's wood near an hour and a half, the liquor operating so much in the head that it rendered my legs useless. Oh, how sensible I am of the goodness of the Divine Providence that I am preserved from harm!

After such occasions his contrition was absolute: 'O, how silly is mankind to delight so much in vanity and transitory joys.'

Speaking as one who has all the usual human failings, and also one or two he has invented for himself, I must say the entry referring to a visit to Whyly in February 1757 has tremendous appeal. The company, which included Mr Porter, the parson, and his wife, supped on chicken and ducks, minced veal, sausages, cold roast goose, chicken pasty and ham. After supper their behaviour was, he wrote:

far from that of serious, harmless mirth; it was downright obstreperous mixed with a great deal of folly and stupidity. Our diversion was dancing or jumping about without a violin or any musick, singing foolish healths, and drinking all the time as it could be well poured down; the parson of the parish was one amongst the mixed multitude.

Finding himself to have had as much liquor as would do him good, he 'slipt away unobserved' at about three o'clock and added, 'Though I was very far from sober I came home, thank God, very safe and well without even tumbling; and Mr French's servant brought my wife home at ten minutes past five!' At six o'clock, just as Mrs Turner was getting into bed, they were roused by the parson's wife on the pretext of wanting some cream of tartar. Mrs Turner went downstairs to be greeted by the parson himself and a Mr Fuller and his wife, 'with a lighted candle and a part of a bottle of wine and a glass'. They went up to Turner's room, but he refused to get out of bed on the grounds of modesty, whereupon they pulled him out 'as the common phrase has it "topsy-turvy" '. Then they made him dance dressed in his wife's petticoats, without shoes or stockings, until they had emptied the wine and a bottle of his beer. At about three o'clock in the afternoon, 'beginning to be a little serious', they found their way to their respective homes.

Thank you, Thomas Turner, for opening a little window onto the social life of rural Sussex in the mid-eighteenth century.

Following the road out of Waldron I walked on until I came to Possingworth Manor House, just past the entrance to which I turned left onto a track that led down past Possingworth Farm Craft Workshop and the Dower House. After half a mile the track joined Hollow Lane onto which I turned right. This brought me out onto the B2192, practically opposite The Blackboys Inn.

Bearing in mind that Belloc wished The Blackboys particularly to be remembered, I bowed to his decree and mounted the steps into the public bar as an act of loyalty. It was five o'clock and, as at Robertsbridge, a group of young men were relaxing after the day's work. Their work-stained lorries, vans and tractors stood in the car park outside, contrasting sharply with the gleaming cars that convey a leisured clientele to visit the saloon bar and restaurant at lunchtimes, for this is a well-known and recommended eatery.

After a pint of bitter, which I considered well earnt after all those miles in the more or less continuous rain, I left and walked up to the Framfield road, and turned west on the last stage of my day's journeying. The local council have made provision at the roadside for foot travellers so, although there was a good deal of traffic, the going was easy, a convenience for which I was very grateful. The rain had at last stopped and the sky was beginning to clear.

Opposite the Hare and Hounds corner in Framfield the approach to the church is flanked by companionable old houses, their tile-hung walls mellowed by the years, and roofs of red tile and Horsham stone draped comfortably about their eaves like a shawl round the shoulders of an elderly lady. Beyond them the ancient lych-gate leads through into the graveyard and the church itself, grey in the evening light with its squat stone tower and Sussex cap of lichened tiles.

For the next half a mile the road has a pavement, but beyond Hammond's Green Farm there is none, so, for those who may wish to do the same as I did and take the quieter more pleasant path, I give the route in some detail. At the signpost

The Blackboys Inn, 'where the little lanes begin'

indicating a right-hand turn to Buxted I walked up the hill under the trees past the brick-built farmhouse and outbuildings. Here a huge tabby cat curled up like an ammonite slept soundly in the barn doorway oblivious of, or merely disinterested in, the farmyard fowls and starlings pecking at spillages of grain within paw's reach.

The unmistakable signs of autumn were apparent in the large log-pile close to the back door and the clump of dahlias shouting their strident colours beside the muted greens of the cabbage patch. But the garden was still yielding well with broccoli, sprouts, parsnips and a long line of runner beans supported on a sturdy structure of hazel rods, paying eloquent tribute to the skills of the gardener and the efficacy of the fertilizer that had come from a large heap in the stable yard.

Almost at the top of the hill a signpost indicated that I had left Framfield behind me, that if I went straight on I would come to Buxted and Hadlow Down, and that a right-hand turn would take me to Framelle Mount, all of which kindly advice I ungratefully ignored and inclined my steps to the left into Sandy Lane. About three hundred yards on I turned right into a lane called Narrow Road, but almost immediately left it for a track forking to the left. The path then went right again just before I reached an iron gate, on which I leant for a while before proceeding. I looked out over the Uck valley, all golden in the evening light, toward Uckfield town. Beyond I could see the long, blue ridge of the South Downs some ten miles distant.

The well-trod path continued amid hazel and chestnut coppices, down through a white-painted 'Stop. Look and Listen' gate and over the railway line, by which time the grey rooftops of Uckfield were coming well into view. In the flat river-meadows a herd of the ubiquitous Friesians were lying contentedly chewing the cud and a flock of about two hundred black-faced Suffolk sheep grazed farther up the river bank. By the bridge over the river Uck is a water-mill of white-painted weatherboard and grey slate. The water trickled pleasantly over the dam beyond which the millpond was like a sheet of glass. Here, too, is Brookside Farm, and in a short distance I was in the eastern outskirts of the town.

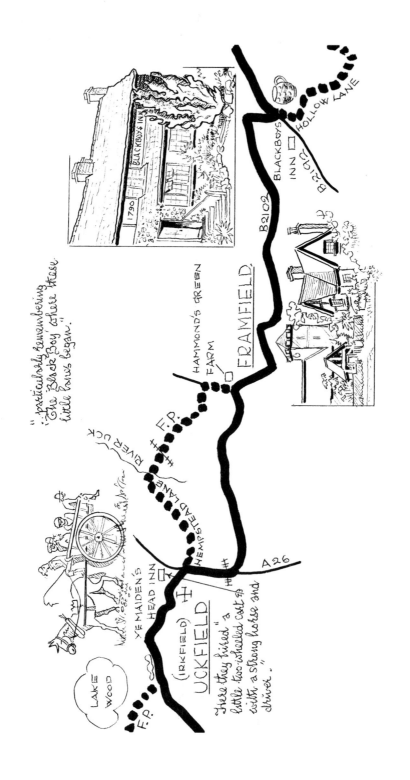

High Street, Uckfield (Irkfield), with Ye Maiden's Head Inn on the right

I followed Hempstead Lane out into Uckfield High Street just south of the sixteenth-century hostelry where I was to find shelter for the night. I cannot say the sign of Ye Maiden's Head beamed a welcome. It portrayed the somewhat sour countenance of the virgin queen herself in a severe mood, heavily bejewelled and complete with ruffle. This ancient inn used to be an important staging post on the oldest Brighton to London coach road, when it ran from the Old Ship Hotel at Brighton via Lewes, Uckfield, Maresfield, East Grinstead, Godstone Green, Croydon and Brixton to London Bridge.

The welcome inside was warm in the extreme and, after a bath and a change of clothing, I dined well on roast lamb, mint sauce and local vegetables, winding up a leisurely meal with ripe Stilton and a most excellent port.

Later I climbed into bed with grateful limbs and lay for a while reflecting on how the day had gone. Then I took *the book* and opened it at the point where the Sailor at the inn at Irkfield had hired 'a little two-wheeled cart with a strong horse and a driver' so that they

> might be driven all those miles through the night to Ardingly, and to the edge of the high woods. . . . out of all this detestable part of the county, which was not made for men, but rather for tourists or foreigners, or London people that had lost their way.

It is, I think, reasonably safe to assume that this took place at Ye Maiden's Head, for at that time it most certainly had the necessary stables, horses, equipage and grooms, and it was gratifying to think that I was so closely following the original route.

I read how they

were driven through the night by cross roads, passing no village except Fletching, until, quite at midnight, we were on the edge of the high woods, and there the driver was paid so much that he could put up and pass the night, but for our part we went on into the trees.

I also read how the Sailor had led them to a little hut in the woods to which he held the key, and where they were to spend the night. Grizzlebeard, being an old man, was to occupy the bench with the rugs, but the other three stretched out on the floor before the log fire that they had lit in 'the great fireplace of brick'.

Before sleep claimed them they talked reflectively and at great length on the worst and the best things in life, a dialogue in which we find Belloc at his best, both erudite and poetic, expounding on philosophical matters with wit, humour and wisdom.

The worst things in life ranged from toothache to the passing of human affection. 'No man who has lost a friend,' said Grizzlebeard, 'need fear death.' The best things in life, thought the Poet, would be a 'mixture wherein should be compounded and intimately mixed great wads of unexpected money, new landscapes and the return of old loves'. While the Sailor, favouring a life of indolence, plumped for being pursued by the Great Three-toed Sloth, 'the most amiable of Hell's emissaries', tickling him forward, lolloping in front of him until finally being overtaken and devoured,

For when I see the grave a long way off, then do I mean to put on slippers and to mix myself a great bowl of mulled wine with nutmegs, and to fill a pipe, and to sit me down in a great arm-chair before a fire of oak or beech, burning in a great hearth, within sound of the Southern Sea.

And as I sit there, drinking my hot wine and smoking my long pipe, and watching the fire, and remembering old storms and landfalls far away, I shall hear the plodding and the paddling and the shuffling and the muffling of that great Sloth, my life's pursuer, and he will butt at my door with his snout, but I shall have been too lazy to lock it, and so shall he come in. Then the great Three-toed Sloth will eat me up and thus shall *I* find the end of my being and have reached the best thing in the world.

But this fascinating conversation was ended summarily by Grizzlebeard who interjected, 'All you young men talk folly. The best thing in the world is sleep',

And having said so much, Grizzlebeard stretched himself upon the bench along one side of the fire, and, pulling his blanket over his head, he would talk to us no more. And we also after a little while, lying huddled in our coats before the blaze, slept hard. And so we passed the hours till morning; now waking in the cold to start a log, then sleeping again. And all night long the wind sounded in the trees.

My eyelids closed on the day, *the book* fell from my hand and the profound sleep that comes to the physically tired and mentally contented man claimed me for the night.

Uckfield to Pease Pottage (20 miles)

At breakfast I deliberated over the means by which I should cover the next stage of the journey. 'Little two-wheeled carts with a strong horse and driver' are at a premium in Uckfield in the present day, and to be driven by car seemed a colourless and feeble substitute calculated to kill on the spot any sense of romance that might be lingering along the way.

The answer came with the third cup of coffee. Through the window I could see Queen Elizabeth swinging gently, almost benignly, against a background of pale blue sky flecked here and there with tiny cotton-wool clouds, which were being driven before a stiffish south-westerly breeze. It was a morning made for walking.

I took the road westward out of Uckfield past the church with its tall, shingled spire reaching up out of the trees in the churchyard. A sprinkling of green leaves on the pavement had been snatched off unseasonably by the gusting wind and rain of the previous day, and I trod them underfoot. After a short while the pavement petered out and, although this is a particularly pretty section of road, winding as it does between cliffs of sandstone rock under a roof of oak and ash, the absence of a footway makes it very much less than comfortable for the pedestrian. There is a constant danger of being either knocked over by the wing of a car or sucked into the slipstream of a hurtling lorry, and I was beginning to wish I had followed the example of my predecessors and ridden through the night. But even in these circumstances my heart was gladdened at the sight of a clump of small yellow balsam (*Impatiens parviflora*) nodding and swaying at the roadside as the traffic flashed past.

This undoubtedly would have been the road taken by our trans-Sussex travellers, but in less than a mile I succumbed to the temptation to abandon the pursuit of historic accuracy in the interests of self-preservation. After passing a lake and a bridge over a bypass road I left the highway and headed north-west onto a footpath, which led me out onto Piltdown Golf Course.

When Belloc wrote about 'setting out under the high morning' this is the sort of day he must have had in mind. The sun was up and riding high, the morning air was as clear as crystal washed clean by yesterday's downpour, and over all the blue dome of the sky arched down to far horizons in every direction. The spirits, too, were high. It was the sort of morning that lifts a man's heart half way to paradise. But just as there are many roads that lead to the kingdom of heaven, so, too, were there a number of paths by which I could cross the open country to Fletching, my next immediate objective. With no predetermined route in mind I set out in a generally north-westerly direction, but influenced to some extent, it must be admitted, by the directional flight of hard-driven golf balls. I finally

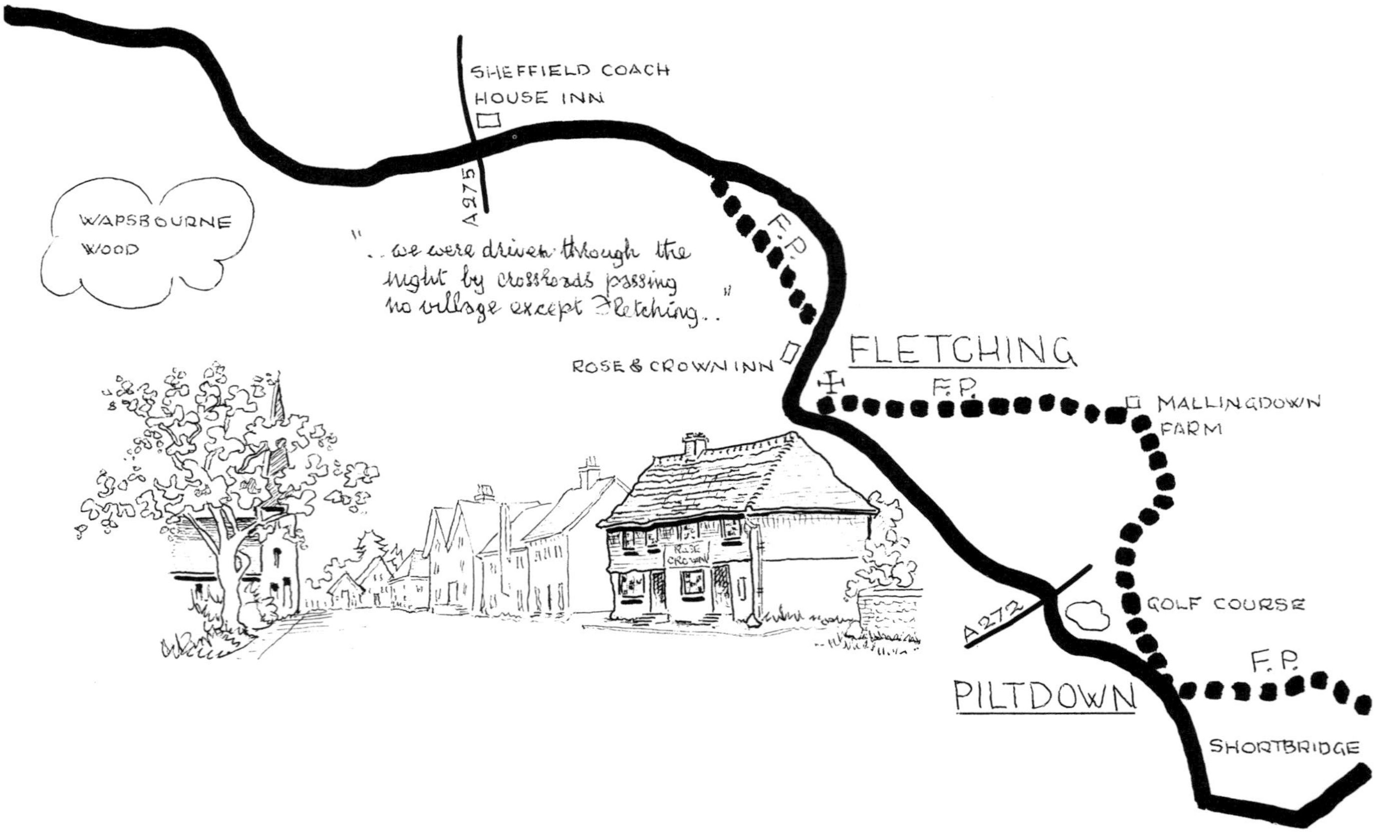

SHEFFIELD COACH
HOUSE INN

A275

WAPSBOURNE
WOOD

F.P.

ROSE & CROWN INN

"... we were driven through the
night by crossroads passing
no village except Fletching ..."

FLETCHING
F.P.

MALLINGDOWN
FARM

A272

GOLF COURSE

PILTDOWN

F.P.

SHORTBRIDGE

emerged by way of the fifteenth green on to the Isfield to Nutley road, which was thankfully practically free of traffic.

At Mallingdown Farm I turned west onto a path towards the steeple of Fletching church, which beckoned like a finger over the brow of a hill about a mile and a half away. Following the not very clearly defined path, muddy in places from yesterday's rains, I was crossing a meadow of deep, lush grass when I spotted two large mushrooms about the size of tea plates, their ample domes gleaming white and irresistible amid the rich green of the pasture. They were really of no practical use to me as I was many miles from my own kitchen, but, bearing in mind how often in the past I have spent many fruitless hours searching for that very same sight, I could not resist them. I stooped and cut them. Their undersides were immaculate and the delicacy of their pale-pink fins undefiled.

There is a certain mystique about mushrooms, something not quite understood, and country lore is full of mysterious allusions to their growing habits and the general aura of magic surrounding them. It is said that they grow in more profusion when the moon is waxing rather than waning; that a mushroom never grows any bigger once it has been seen by human eyes; that you should be sure to inscribe a cross on the top of the severed stalk left in the ground in order to ensure that future searches will be well rewarded. Certain varieties of fungi are known to induce hallucinations and have somewhat sinister connotations, but these were the good old down-to-earth natives that would only feel at home in a panful of sizzling rashers. I carried them with care, for I was no more than half a mile from the village where I felt sure I would find someone glad to have them.

I emerged on to the road through Church Farm, idly wondering if I would have the luck to meet the ghost, or at least a descendant, of Peter Dynot, a glover of Fletching, notorious for being an associate of Jack Cade back in the fifteenth century, and of whom I had read the previous day at Heathfield. But the first person I saw was an elderly man sedately free-wheeling past on a large, black bicycle. Of above average height and sturdy build, he sat bolt upright in the saddle with only a perfunctory hold on the handlebars, and relying on the slight downward gradient of the road for forward impetus, which was only just sufficient, I would have thought, for him to maintain his balance. He wore a blue serge suit and black boots, and with his head tonsured by nature with only a fringe of white hair at ear level, which contrasted sharply with his sunburnt crown and countenance, he had the composure and dignity of an Edwardian gentleman being driven to church in a brougham and pair.

'Morning,' I called.

''Ow do,' he replied.

'Fair ol' day.'

'Yeah,' he said as his keen eyes swivelled to the mushrooms I was holding. 'Got a couple o' mesheroons then, I see.'

'That's right. I found 'em up in the field yonder. I'm looking for a home for them.'

'Wal,' he said, his magisterial air dissolving in an instant as he dismounted with remarkable agility for one of his years, 'you wun't 'ave to look no further.'

He had been out searching for mushrooms for the last hour or two with markedly less success than I, and a basket strapped to the handlebars of his bicycle contained half a dozen or so small buttons, the sum of his morning's

Fletching village around the turn of the century. '. . . we were driven through the night . . . passing no village except Fletching'

efforts. When he added my contribution his stock went up by four or five hundred per cent and I could see I was a friend for life.

Fred was a man of the old school who had lived all of his life in Fletching. I mentioned my own farming background, incorrectly assuming that he had similar roots.

'No,' he answered, 'I've bin keeperin' all my time.' He expanded on this theme later over a pint of mild ale in the bar of the Rose and Crown in the High Street: 'When I was a li'l ol' boy this pub was kept by three sisters and their names was Faith, Hope and Charity – that was their Christian names, like. They 'ad thirteen cats between 'em – ah, an' they was all three of 'em spinsters, look.' I ventured the somewhat trite observation that their names might more suitably have been Faith, Hope and Chastity. 'Yeah,' returned Fred with a knowing look, '*should* 'ave bin.'

We sat in the part of the room that had once been the public bar, close to a wide inglenook fireplace built of sandstone blocks, black with smoke and shiny from many years of wear and tear. The stones at shoulder height on the left-hand pier were deeply etched with roughly vertical crevices up to half an inch deep, giving them the appearance of the bark of an ancient oak tree.

'That's where the ol' fellers used t' sharp their jack-knives,' said Fred.

Do you know what! I've seen an ol' chep sittin' in that chair there with a sack o' dead moles on the floor aside of 'im, takin' 'em out, skinnin' of 'em on 'is knee an' chuckin' the naked carcasses on the fire. They didn' 'alf used t' sizzle, I can tell y' – and stink!

In those few words Fred had painted a picture that took him back to his boyhood, but which also conjured up for me a vision of country pub interiors as they had been before the motor-borne invasion of the countryside in the 1930s.

If ever there was a man who could be said to be the child of his environment, that man was Fred. Now in his advanced seventies, he had spent his entire working life in the woodlands, the meadows and brooksides of mid-Sussex. The badger's tracks, the squawk of the pheasant and the weed-draped haunts of the speckled trout were an open book to him, and the unfolding seasons were his creed. He spoke the language of the wild woods, and the buoyant airs of the great outdoors were all about him. His ebullience and zest for living were like a morning breeze and his wisdom was that of the midnight owl. He told me of his early days in the village:

I was born in the Queen's Hotel, Eastbourne, where my mother was working at the time, but I was brought up in Fletching an' I've bin here ever since, like. I started keeperin' in 1928 when I was sixteen an' the first suit o' clothes I had come from the local tailor up the street here. Twenty-nine pounds that cost. Stockin's, boots, buckskin breeches an' a nice Scotch tweed jacket with breast an' side pockets – a bit like a Norfolk jacket it was. Yeah, twenty-nine pounds – that was a lot o' money in them days, look.

I worked for Lord Sheffield at Sheffield Park an' it was a very big estate. There was fourteen groundsmen, twelve kitchen-garden staff and twenty farmhands. We had six gamekeepers an' a boy as well as the head-keeper. We used to have gentlemen guns flown in from Switzerland, France and America to come an' shoot. Oh yeah, it was a very big affair.

My father worked as a coalman from the yard at the back of the Griffin down the road. He had two horses and a waggon and delivered bags o' coal round the village. He would pick a load o' coal up from Sheffield Park station in the mornin', an' then, perhaps, in the aft'noon he'd have t' wash the horses t' get the coal-dust off 'em an' get ready for another job which was a very different kettle o' fish. He'd rush home an' have a quick wash hisself an' then change – wal, just his trousers, like, he wouldn't have a bath or anything like that. Then he'd put on one o' them stiff shirt-fronts, you know, a dickie; hitch the ol' horses up to the hearse an' go off to a funeral. Then in the evenin' he might have t' put one o' the horses in a trap an' go off to pick someone up from the railway station. He wasn't very often idle, I can tell y'.

When I was about seventeen I'd have t' go out with a .410 shotgun and walk the stubbles where they'd put the ol' dung-heaps ready for spreading. That's where the ol' hares used t' sit. They'd make a little hole in the dung an' stick their arses back in it an' sit there in the warm. I always had to get four for the mansion down here, an' I tell you what, four damn gurt hares wanted a bit o' carryin' home for a boy o' that age with two an' a half or three mile to go.

When I was learnin' I used t' go out with the head-keeper, Pritchard, ferretin'. We'd leave about nine in the mornin' with about a hundred nets an' we always reckoned to have about a hundred rabbits before dinner at one. Rabbits! You've never seen anythin' like it in your life. There wasn't no stubble on the headlands; they used t' eat it right down, corn, stubble, the lot! They wanted a bit o' carryin', too. You'd have a damn gurt stick over y' shoulder with fifteen in front an' another fifteen behind – an' then some in the bag an' some in the poacher's pocket o' y' jacket. Ol' Pritchard used t' carry 'em home paunch an' all an' that did make 'em heavy. We used to *stagger* home with 'em.

I had two disasters out ferretin'. One day I was out on me own an' I laid the nets an' put the ferret in, an' waited. Wal, nothin' happens for a while an' I couldn't hear him movin' about down there, so I thinks to meself, 'I reckon he's laid up.' They would sometimes catch a rabbit down in the hole an' lay up an' start eatin' it. There was some leaves in the mouth o' the hole where I'd put him so I scratched 'em out o' the way; got down on me hands and knees an' I thought I could hear him movin' about just a little way in. I got down real close an' put me face right in the hole to see if I could see him. An' that bleddy thing whipped out at me an' clamped his teeth right through there, look (he pointed to the septum between his nostrils), an' he hung there. I grabs hold of him an' pulls on the back of his neck till at last he let go. I was covered in blood, look, an' it didn't half make my eyes water. Anyway, I put him in the bag an' went home without a single rabbit.

A couple o' weeks later the same ferret lays up again. I had about forty nets out on an open bank. I stuck me spade in the ground an' put me ear to the handle to see if I could hear him – but it was all quiet. Then I thought I saw some leaves move a little way inside the hole so I gets down on me hands and knees. But I don't go too close, I can tell you. I just put me ear close t' the hole to listen an' that bleddy ferret leapt out an' stuck his teeth right through the lobe of my earhole. I jumped up and yanked him off – bleedin' like a stuck pig I was. Then I threw him down on the ground, picked up me twelve-bore an' let him have both barrels. He went sky high in pieces an' that was the last I ever see of him.

That was the only ferret I ever had any trouble with an' I've handled enough in my time. I used t' breed 'em an' I would put me hand in the hutches an' stroke 'em an' roll 'em over; there'd be six in here an' eight in there, but I never had no trouble with 'em – not till this one.

We used to have some big pheasant shoots with ninety to a hundred beaters. They used t' get a pint bottle of brown ale, two bits o' bread and a large chunk of cheese, and two big sausages. Then they was paid two shillings and sixpence [12½p] for the day on top o' their wages. At the end o' the winter we used to pen up the birds in runs surrounded by six foot o' wire-nettin' for laying and hatchin'. We used t' band 'em with rubber bands, but only one wing, look, so they could fly round the pen but not up over the wire. We also brought some birds in from the hatcheries.

But keeperin' is hard now, the poachers work from cars. They'll go out six in a car and drop one off to fire off a few rounds as a decoy to attract the attention of the keeper, while three or four mile up the road the other five are gettin' their bags full. Then they've got a silent method. They have a long rod in sections like a fishing rod about twenty foot long and they hang a tin in the end and put a little carbide in it. Then they put some water on it – or if they haven't got any water they piddles on it – then they raise it up under the head of a roosting bird and the ol' gas goes up there, my boy, an' in less than a minute he'll fall off the perch and come down bang on the ground at their feet. They have t' be middlin' quick off the mark to grab him or he'll come round again in a couple o' minutes.

We had five big lakes on the estate and plenty o' wild duck. But that was never let out to anyone. But if, say, some ol' duke flew in from Switzerland with his two sons an' stayed in the mansion down here they might want to go fishing. There was some monstrous pike down there. I've seen a boat ten or twelve foot long and four or five foot wide with a couple o' chaps in it being towed round that lake by a pike hooked on a live minnow bait. Then when he was exhausted they'd get him in the boat with a gaff. Over three foot long an' as thick through as a lorry tyre – an' bleddy near black with old age.

We use t' have some rare ol' singsongs in this ol' bar on a Saturday night. We all used t' drink mild ale in them days an' it was served up in jugs and passed round to fill your pots. Then when it was your turn to pay you just filled up the jug. If anyone came in an' ordered whisky you'd think, wal, he must be a bit of a lardy-dah, he must be a farmer or something. Whisky was right out of our depth.

Ol' 'Eggie' Weller used to sing a song called 'The Crockery Ware':

> After gaining her consent
> Straightway up to bed they went,
> She placed him in an old armchair
> And underneath some crockeryware.
> With a right for the ridy-vo,
> Right for the ridy-vo.
>
> Then Johnny got groping in the dark
> Thinking he was up to a lark,
> He blundered up against a bleddy old chair
> And arse-overhead went the crockeryware.
> With a right for the ridy-vo,
> Right for the ridy-vo.

It was a beguiling experience to sit there listening to old Fred spinning his yarns and telling of the things he had seen over the years there in that very room. But at last I bade him goodbye and walked on up the street toward Nutley, with the strains of 'The Crockery Ware' running through my head.

At the top end of the street, opposite Atherall's Farm, I came to a white-painted gate on the left bearing a notice: 'Attested Friesian Herd'. I left the road to follow a path across an open field in a north-westerly direction. The herd referred to comprised about thirty heifers, lying down contentedly away to the south, but which, on seeing me, got up and followed. They probably thought I had something for them in the way of fodder, for they crowded closely in on my heels and occasionally one would nudge me in the backside with her muzzle as if to remind me that they were hungry. When I got to the gate on the far side they jostled me into the corner and I had to shove them back to get the gate open. They were in no way vicious or threatening, merely inquisitive and obstinate, but it took some effort to get the gate open. Anyone not entirely at ease in bovine company would be well advised to stick to the road by way of Splayne's Green. It will add only a matter of yards to the distance travelled. I joined the road again at the entrance to Splayne's Green Farm and resumed a westerly direction.

Westward, westward, ever westward. There is something absolutely right and proper about travelling in a westerly direction. It feels right because it is the way of nature. Henry Thoreau held this view over a hundred years ago and, allowing for the fact that he was a full-blown patriotic American, whose instincts would have been conditioned to some extent by the great western drive made by his pioneer countrymen across their newly acquired country, he was still convinced that more subtle forces were at work. He wrote:

> Every sunset which I witness inspires me with the desire to go to a West as distant and as fair as that into which the sun goes down. He appears to migrate westward daily and tempts us to follow him. He is the Great Western Pioneer whom the nations follow. We dream all night of those mountain ridges in the horizon, though they may be of vapour only, which were last gilded by his rays.

Grizzlebeard had said much the same sort of thing to the Poet in his invitation to join them at Cade Street.

The sun is certainly a good companion to the west-bound traveller. He sends you off with a warm pat on the back in early morning, whispers words of encouragement over your left shoulder at noon, and, going on ahead, he turns to greet you home with a smile when the day is over and the trek done.

The morning sun at that moment was filtering down through the foliage of the trees, throwing dappled shadows, which danced on the road ahead. The wild growth in the roadside hedgerows was still vigorous and long, and searching trailers of wild hops festooned the hawthorn. Only the silver birches with their small leaves beginning to turn a lemon-yellow, showed any real sign of the approaching fall, and here and there scabious and rosebay willow-herb were still blooming, though most of the latter bore at least some of their characteristic fluffy seed-heads. The bracken, too, was beginning to assume the mature look of late summer. Some of the older oaks must have been standing here when The Four Men rumbled past in that cart on their journey through the night in 1902. The road was quiet with very little traffic.

At North Hall Farm in a shallow dip I crossed a little bridge over a stream of water the colour of pale sherry, and soon afterwards came to a junction where the lane crosses the Lewes to East Grinstead road. Just to the north of the crossroads, lying back from the main road, is the Sheffield Coach House, once called the Sheffield Arms, a large brick-built hotel with adjoining stables. Fred had told me that it was originally built to accommodate the overflow of gentlemen and horses from the mansion on the occasions of large hunting and shooting parties.

There is an expansive green in front of the buildings, with well-established oak and sweet chestnut trees and a white-painted dovecote, which houses a dozen or so white fan-tailed pigeons, which peck about at the crumbs under the tables put there for the convenience of customers, or strut up and down on the red-tiled roofs nearby. Inside in the Dickens Bar the landlord told me that a few years back the hotel had been run by a Mr Dickens, a great-great-grandson of Charles Dickens, who had furnished the room with Cecil Aldin prints of Dickensian scenes and other memorabilia of his illustrious ancestor, which still adorn the walls today. I took sufficient food and drink to carry me on to Ardingly.

Back in the lane I followed on in the same direction where, on the western side of the main road, it had become Ketche's Lane. Here it was no more than ten feet wide, and there was no sound but the plodding of my boots on the road surface and the occasional shriek of a cock pheasant, like the scream of a dry axle crying out for grease. I became more and more convinced that this was the road Belloc had taken, and if he travelled along it today he would find it precisely the same as in his day. Following its slightly sinuous and gently undulating course, I soon came to the eponymous farm from which the lane took its name. One imagines that Ketche's Farm was the only feature of importance on this long byway in days gone by and, the truth to tell, nothing so far as I could see has changed in that respect. In the farmyard there is one large barn of tarred weatherboard on lower courses of brick that is pretty old, but the remainder of the outbuildings and the house are of later years. It is still isolated and obviously calls for adequate security measures. 'BEWARE', announced a prominent notice in red lettering, 'DOBERMAN GUARD DOG', followed by an exclamation mark by way of emphasis. I quickly went on my way in a quiet and orderly manner, not wishing to give the canine sentry the slightest reason to prove his effectiveness. I didn't even see or hear him – the notice was enough for me.

I walked on and my shadow trotted along dutifully at my side, bumping along on the hedgerows, popping into every open gateway and drawing himself out to his full length on the surface of open fields. Now short, now long, he is always with me, at least when the weather is fine.

I came to an open space of ground at the top of a rise where the wind was more noticeable and a large oak tree lay grounded, just another victim of the great hurricane. On one of its exposed roots a large fungus flourished. The multi-bulbous form of its upper surface was similar to a bullock's kidney, but the colours, ranging from sulphur yellow through orange and red to purple and magenta were dazzling in the bright sunlight. It was a good fourteen inches across and, having since looked it up, I think it must have been a specimen of *Polyporus sulphureus*. In the corner of the field a patch of giant hogweed some five or six feet high had run to seed, the individual plants waving their heads in the wind like skeletal umbrellas.

At Freshfield Crossways, where the garden belonging to the cottage of that name was bright with salvias, asters, nicotiana and sunflowers, I consulted the map. What a practical and spiritual aid a good map is on a walk like this. It points the way, saving many unnecessary footsteps, supplies up-to-date information on footpaths and rights of way, and, in giving the ancient names of highways and farmsteads still in use, preserves something of the past and stimulates our senses of history and romance. What dreams can be woven around names like Wildboar Bridge, Lower Sheriff Farm, Skein Winders, Laundry Cottage, Hangman's Acre and Butterbox Farm.

Under the Bluebell Railway and over Cockhaise Brook I came to Cockhaise Mill Farm, a group of attractive buildings with strong brick and stone walls, some white weatherboard and mellow tiled roofs spotted with lichen. Part of the mill is now open as a farm shop, offering a wide range of excellent comestibles, from venison to woodcock, and guinea fowl to smoked salmon, not to mention the large, chunky, succulent pork sausages.

A few hundred yards on, opposite the entrance to Cockhaise Farm, stands an ancient and noble oak tree. Its hollow trunk, a good ten feet across at its widest, supports mighty, tortuous limbs that twist and writhe up into the dark green recesses of its huge canopy of summer foliage.

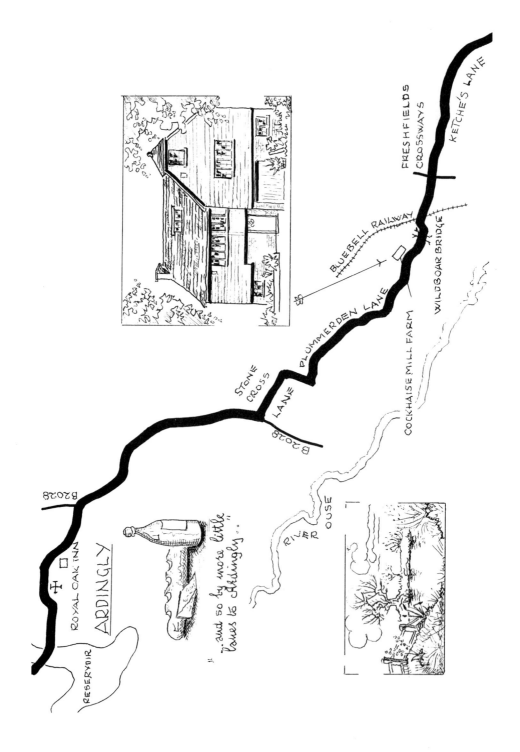

RESERVOIR

ROYAL OAK INN

ARDINGLY

B2028

B2028

STONE CROSS

LANE

PLUMMERDEN LANE

BUEBELL RAILWAY

FRESHFIELDS CROSSWAYS

KETCHE'S LANE

WILDBOAR BRIDGE

COCKHAISE MILL FARM

RIVER OUSE

"...and so by more little lanes to Ardingly..."

At a three-road junction north-east of East Mascall's I took the right-hand turn into Plummerden Lane and, after a mile or so of steady climbing, I topped a rise that afforded splendid views: north and east over undulating, fairly heavily wooded country in bright sunshine; and south and west to the distant Downs in dark cloud shadow. About six miles away to the south-east I could see the spire of a church, which I took to be Fletching church. A right turn into Keysford Lane and another left into Stonecross Lane brought me out on to the B2028.

Here I left behind the gentle, slow-moving atmosphere that still lingers in these peaceful lanes and was suddenly thrust into the frantic world of present-day road travel. Cars hurtled past in both directions. It is a hair-raising piece of road for the walker and the only consolation was that I had to follow it for only a little over half a mile before a sidewalk offered safe passage into Ardingly.

Sitting on the green opposite The Royal Oak Inn I turned the pages of *the book*, trying to determine just where our mentor and his friends had left the cart, paid the driver and taken to the woods, but the details were imprecise. Determined to keep the walk as much in character as possible, I went into the village stores and purchased a small French loaf, some strong cheddar cheese and a half-bottle of Chablis. The metric standards by which such things are sold nowadays, and to which we are only now, after several years, reluctantly becoming accustomed (400 grammes of bread, 227 grammes of cheese and 37.5 centilitres of wine) with their continental connotations, added just enough Frenchified influence to ensure the Bellocian nature of the meal, and I sat in the afternoon sunshine enjoying a repast that was satisfactorily suitable to the occasion.

Out past the church I followed the road through the trees with occasional outcroppings of sandstone on either side and down the steep incline to the bridge over what is now the Ardingly Reservoir. When I walked this road in 1950, many

Ardingly High Street, looking south, early 1900s. '. . . we might be driven all those miles through the night to Ardingly, and to the edge of the high woods'

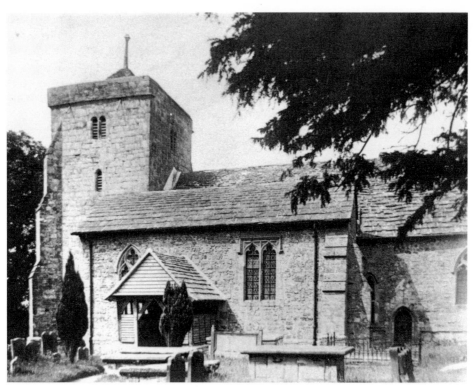

Ardingly church

years before the dam was built just above the college, the intimate little Ardingly Brook babbled under a small, stone-arched bridge where wrens nested in the crevices. Today all that is drowned beneath the surface of this wide expanse of water, which covers many acres.

Up the other side I ignored the turning to Balcombe on my left and took the right-hand fork northwards along a very narrow road, between hedgerows and trees that met overhead in the most picturesque manner. A signpost indicated that I was on the road to Turner's Hill and East Grinstead. It was very quiet and my approach disturbed a group of small rabbits playing in the sun at the roadside. About two miles further on I left the road over a stile and followed a path along the south-western boundary of Downside Wood, a coniferous plantation. There were good views of Worth Abbey to the north. Originally Paddockhurst, it was one of the many beautiful big houses in this area, which was developed by the first Lord Cowdray. It became the home of the Benedictine monks about sixty years ago.

Being in this vicinity brought to mind the occasion one Boxing Day morning when I was walking over Staplefield Green towards the Victory Inn, and noticed on the green immediately in front of the inn a group of about twenty people intent on watching some game that was in progress. It was a cold morning and a pallid sun threw long shadows across the frost-whitened grass. As I drew nearer I could see some of them blowing their fists and stamping their feet to bring the circulation back into their frozen extremities. Stiff brown ploughlands ran right up to the hedge at the side of the inn and a seasonal touch was added by a holly tree laden with bright scarlet berries.

On the green were two semi-spherical mounds of dark brown, clay soil heaped up about eighteen yards apart, and each had a sprig of holly stuck in the top. They were about two feet across at the base and stood a foot or so high, looking like two enormous Christmas puddings one placed at each end of the pitch. The players each threw two iron quoits weighing three to four pounds, and the object was to place them as near as possible to, or on, the pudding, the prime goal being to ring the sprig of holly, an unlikely event at that distance. The scoring was similar to a game of bowls and decisions in matters of close measurements were made by a man who acted as a referee and followed the game closely, first from one end and then from the other. After each set he would wipe the mud from the quoits with a cloth and shout out the scores, sending out his breath like steam on the cold morning air.

On a trestle table laden with partly consumed pots of beer was a blackboard on which another man chalked the scores. The spectators watched keenly, and those who drew too close were sometimes splattered with mud as the heavy quoits fell flat onto the squelchy ground or, at times, onto the pudding itself, which, as the frost thawed, became surrounded by water like a moat. There was a great deal of banter and good-natured leg-pulling, and the whole thing proceeded in a very light-hearted and friendly manner. There were five players in each team and when the game was over – won, if I remember correctly, by the visiting team by eleven sets to nine – we all trooped into the inn parlour.

Inside, the beams were decorated with greenery and tinsel, and a log fire blazed in the open hearth. With glasses replenished the company soon thawed out, and the room was filled with the buzz and hum of convivial chat and laughter. The men smoked cigars and sported new neck-ties, and the women wore pretty head scarves and were redolent with exotic perfume, all of which only hours before had been taken from their gift wrap. Soon the air was thick with smoke.

Vic, the landlord, told me it was an annual event:

Every summer Staplefield plays Warninglid, our neighbouring village, at cricket on the green out there. It's been going on for years and has become a sort of local Derby. About sixteen years ago we found ourselves at the end of the season with one game each to our credit and no time to arrange a decider because of the dark evenings. Someone suggested that we should meet here next Boxing Day morning to settle the matter by playing quoits, and we've kept it up ever since.

They now have a challenge trophy of a wooden quoit mounted on a base on which each year's winners are inscribed.

Presently the door opened and in came about eighteen hearty-looking monks, well wrapped or hooded against the cold. They had walked the seven miles from Worth Abbey and came into the friendly fug of the bar, mingling among us with their eyes bright and clear and their cheeks flushed with the winter air. I was struck by the ease with which the two factions merged into one company – us from our various little founts of ungodliness; they from their bastion of sanctity – all at one under that tiny, hospitable roof in the merry mood of the season. It was like pouring a bucket of pure well-water into a perfumed bath. But there we were,

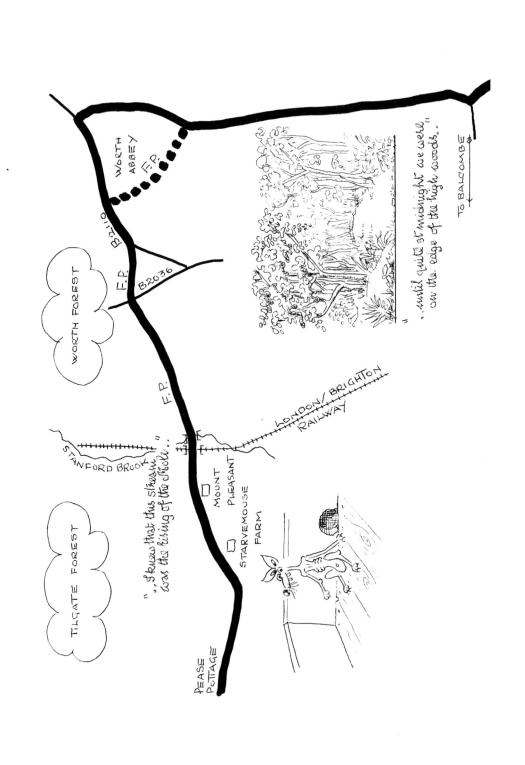

WORTH ABBEY

F.P.

B2110

F.P.

WORTH FOREST

B2036

TO BALCOMBE

"..until quite at midnight we were on the edge of the high woods.."

F.P.

LONDON/BRIGHTON RAILWAY

STANFORD BROOK

TILGATE FOREST

"..I knew that this stream was the rising of the Mole.."

MOUNT PLEASANT

STARVEMOUSE FARM

PEASE POTTAGE

the sacred on equal terms with the secular; the dedicated hobnobbing with the dissolute in complete harmony.

The monks then seated themselves at a long table and ate packed lunches, which they had brought with them, rinsing the food down with pints of bitter. It was a classic scene with scriptural overtones. But this was a holiday occasion, a foray, it could be said, into the knock-about world of ordinary men and women, and privileges were granted. With the meal over those that chose to lit up pipes or cigarettes, and in one instance a long corona-corona Havana cigar, and this juncture was marked by the arrival of Wallace, the Prior himself, who had been driven down by car. He was greeted with a cheer and offered the seat of honour at the centre of the company.

Then they began to sing carols and Christmas songs, starting off with 'The Twelve Days of Christmas'. They sang tunefully and with a brisk enthusiasm that was a joy to hear, and we all joined in to the best of our ability. When it came to 'Ding, Dong Merrily on High' the holy men went cascading down the 'glorias' with professional ease that left the more worldly among us sadly out of breath. This was followed by 'Good King Wenceslas', a large, dark-haired blacksmith of a man taking the King's part in a resounding bass, and answered by an ascetic-looking young man called Simon singing that of the Page in a clear, steady falsetto. Through the clapping and cheers that applauded their efforts at the end I heard a voice, it may have been the Prior's: 'Canto for you next week, Simon.'

When it was time to leave we all shook hands outside, then I watched as the monks receded across the green on their walk back to the Abbey, and to a mode of life so markedly different from that of those whose company they had shared for the past hour or so. Before they disappeared into the trees on the opposite side of the green, one or two of them turned to wave their staffs in farewell for another year to the world and all its wickedness. It was a memorable occasion.

Less than half a mile westward on the main road (the B2110), which was well provided with flat green verges very convenient for walkers, I took a track on my right marked Public Bridleway through an open white gateway, close to a red-brick house and in the general direction of Whitely Hill. I was now well into the forest country and very close to where the Four Men took to the road after spending the night in the little wooden hut.

> By this time we were all upon the forest path again, turning this way and that as the Sailor might lead us. Sometimes we crossed a great ride without turning down it, and once the broad high road. But we went straight across that.

I also went straight across it – having due regard to the prevailing traffic conditions, of course – for this is the busy B2036 which was once one of the Brighton to London coach roads passing through Cuckfield, Balcombe, Worth, Pound Hill and Horley. The bridleway continues on the other side in the same direction through land thickly afforested on either side with various trees: oak, silver birch, sweet chestnut and assorted conifers.

Although Belloc took this diversion to the north to avoid passing through the conurbations that had grown up within easy reach of the railway line to London, it quite fortuitously brings us up into a part of the county that is highly individual in character and very lovely. The heavily wooded sandstone ridges and stream-bearing valleys of this forest area were described by Horsfield as 'Much undulated with hill and dale, though altogether elevated above the general level of the Weald. . . . with boskey dingles and romantic glades, which in every direction meet the eye.'

I walked on freely along the public path where Belloc had blatantly trespassed:

we passed many signs where it said that any common man found in these woods would be imprisoned, and somewhere it said that anyone not rich and yet wandering here might find themselves killed by engines.

This sounds as if spring-loaded guns and mantraps were still in use, but I could have wandered at will quite legally to the right or left of the trackway with no hindrance to free passage but fallen trees blocking the path. This is one way in which the countryside has been improved in the last ninety years.

About a mile further on in Tilgate Forest the track led me into a leafy dell bathed in green reflected light, with the occasional rapier-shaft of sunlight striking down through the foliage overhead, which blotted out the sky. The path dropped down until at its lowest point a simple footbridge carried it over a narrow stream of clear water meandering to the north. I stood on the bridge for a moment or two, and there was no sound save the trickle of water beneath me and the leaves rustling overhead. A boskey dingle, indeed.

We came to a bottom through which a stream ran, and then I knew that this stream was the rising of the Mole, and that we were in Tilgate. Then I said to my companions: 'Now the woods smell of home!' . . . When we had rested ourselves a moment in this glade we followed the Sailor again by a path which presently he left, conducting us with care through the untouched underwood, until we came to a hedge and there across the hedge was the great main road and Pease Pottage close at hand.

Crossing a brick-built bridge over the railway line the path climbs fairly steeply, the ground thickly strewn with fallen pine needles and soft to the feet. The track becomes a made-up road after a short while and leads past two small farms on the left the names of which seem to sum up the fluctuating fortunes of the farming world. Mount Pleasant rubs shoulders with Starvemouse Farm.

It was hereabouts that Belloc turned to his companions and

asked them severally whether they had any curse on them which forbade them to drink ale of a morning. This all three of them denied, so we went into the Swan (which in those days I say again was the old inn), and we drank ale.

I crossed over the relentless two-way flow of the M23 by way of a flyover (an experience that would have left Belloc speechless with rage and bewilderment), and there straight ahead was the Swan. Well, no, not exactly – the present-day building has been extended and altered beyond recognition, the road layout completely changed, and it is now called the James King Restaurant and Public House. I went in for a drink.

Belloc was at pains to point out that in 1902 they went into the *old* inn, which indicates that by the time he wrote the book nine years later it had already seen some alteration. When I went there in 1950 very little had changed, I would have thought, in forty years. It was a typical, unprepossessing roadside pub, and at that time the main Brighton to London road ran right past the door, and so far as I could see the so-called passing trade was precisely that and therefore non-existent. The room was sparsely furnished with match-boarded walls, bare floorboards, and a varnished and grained counter. Its name then was the Black Swan.

In the James King I sat over a pint of bitter thinking of these things and looking around me at the decor, which was about par for the course in these days. Fitted carpets, concealed lighting, heavy curtains and comfortably upholstered chairs, and I was uncomfortably aware that Mr B. would not have approved. At least I had the satisfaction of studying some splendid photographs of the old inn displayed on the walls.

I walked a short distance down the road that once carried all of the traffic between Brighton and London and at this point is no more than nine paces wide. In the bar of The Grapes Inn a large, jovial-looking man sat with an enormous gin and tonic in a pint glass on the table beside him. He was middle-aged and of muscular build, with a fine head of black hair brushed straight back from his forehead, and he wore a colourful neckerchief gathered at the throat with a broad ring of gold. He was well composed and of a genial disposition, and there was a relaxed air about him that at once made me feel at ease in his company. We got into conversation and the chat turned this way and that before we found common ground.

He was one of five sons in a family renowned in this corner of Sussex for their singing, and they still got together from time to time for an evening of fun and, of course, singing. The songs they sang were traditional and very old, and they sang

The Black Swan Inn, Pease Pottage, where they drank ale

them unaccompanied with improvised harmonies, as was the mode until the early years of this century. They learnt most of their songs from their mother, who was still alive.

A couple of drinks later we started to swap songs *sotto voce*, and the evening slipped on the familiar garments of good fellowship in friendly surroundings. Later he took me to his home nearby and I met Josephine, his mother.

Josephine carried her years lightly. As diminutive in stature as her son was huge, she retained the features of a pretty woman, with hazel eyes still capable of sparkling with mischief. Her hair, greying now but still plentiful, was scraped back severely and it was apparent that, though she was blessed with a sense of humour, she was a person of determined character. Her looks owed nothing to the artifices of the hairdresser or beautician and she spurned the use of cosmetics. In fact, she told me that she thought vanity was a sin.

She and the twentieth century had been born at the same time. They were in their teens together, had weathered the trials and tribulations of middle age and now, after a long life, including two world wars, of the two, Mabs, as she was affectionately called, wore her age the more graciously. She had the energy and mental agility of someone half her age.

A bottle of wine was opened and the singing started in earnest, the *voces* no longer *sotto*. When Gordon, for such was his name, embarked on a song it was like the launching of a battleship, and he sailed full ahead with all guns blazing. Great, majestic bass notes came booming up from the depths of his chest and carried the song along indomitably to the haven of its conclusion and the final chorus. He was a determined and compelling singer if ever I heard one:

> Our bugle sounds truce for the night cloud was lowered,
> The sentinel stars kept their watch from the sky,
> And thousands had sunk to the ground overpowered,
> The weary to sleep and the wounded to die . . .

His song breathed the pulse of life into history and echoed back to the Battle of Salamanca, 1812.

Mab's voice matched her frame the same as her son's matched his – it was light and true. 'Sing us a really old one, mother,' said Gordon, 'you know, the one that used to make me cry when I was a little chap.' The thought that he had ever been a little chap was difficult to accommodate, and that a song had ever caused him to cry strained credulity to impossible limits, but I was to learn differently.

'O, yes,' replied Mabs, 'he used to say, "sing the one that always makes me cry, Mum, and when I start crying you stop." ' Then after a couple of trial notes to get the pitch, she sang in a clear and confident voice:

> It's of a jolly farmer come out of Gloucestershire,
> And all his full intentions were to court some lady fair,
> Whose eyes shone like the morning star,
> Whose hair was crimped and gay,
> She had grace within her face,
> That was mixed with modesty.

During the song I noticed Gordon surreptitiously wipe the corner of one eye, but Mabs sang on to the end.

Mabs talked about her early life. She was born on a farm near Wivelsfield and as a small girl had to do all of the jobs that were demanded of country children in those days. She told me about the first time she milked a cow and was awarded a box round the ear for her pains. Proud of her achievement she placed the foaming bucket at the back of the cow and trotted off to tell her father of her success. But when they returned the unthinkable had happened and she felt the weight of her father's heavy hand at the side of her head. 'Well,' she said, when she was telling me the story, 'how did I know the ol' cow was going to muck in the bucket?'

She also told me that her mother was a tall woman with black hair and pale blue eyes that betrayed her Hibernian ancestry. The old lady had many stories about her childhood and used to make Mabs' flesh creep with the account of how her great-grandmother had been sold into bondage on the streets of Dublin. She knew a host of songs, many of them from Ireland, and she was always singing as she went about her household tasks. That is how Mabs learnt so many of the songs she still remembers and sings so well today.

In due course we sat down to a table and had a delicious supper of cold ham, salad and pickles with another bottle of wine, and their liberal hospitality extended to offering me a bed for the night – an offer I accepted with alacrity.

Before I switched off the bedside lamp on a long day, remarkable for its insight into the beauties of the Sussex rural scene and the warmth and generosity of its people, I scribbled the concluding stanzas of the verse I had started the day before.

And has the evening found you there
Where friendly faces beam
Around a glowing, tavern fire
That makes your toe-caps steam?

And have you then been well regaled
With bacon, bread and beer,
And made the evening loud with song,
With laughter and good cheer?

And have you stretched your weary limbs
Between clean sheets at night,
And soundly slept beneath deep thatch
Till morning's early light?

Then you have precious memories
A kindly fate has given,
And you'll make them green with envy
When you tell 'em so in Heaven.

DAY THREE

Pease Pottage to Ashurst (17 miles)

I awoke next morning to the chattering of sparrows under the eaves, and the first word that came floating into my not yet entirely lucid mind was 'Golier' – just the one word, 'Golier'. I am not certain about the pronunciation; I am not even sure how to spell it – Golier or Goliere. Arthur Beckett spelt it with a terminal 'e'; Belloc without.

Belloc refers to an ancient song called 'Golier' as the national anthem of Sussex, but the details are maddeningly vague. We get a tantalizing glimpse on the title-page of *the book*: just a couple of bars of music – seven notes, no more – and the words 'I will sing Golier.' Then he touches on it again when talking of Jack Fuller of Brightling making his way to Westminster in his coach and six horses: 'and, God willing, as he went he sang the song, "Golier, Golier!" '. In fact, the most of this song we get at any time is in his account of a meal in bucolic company at an inn in West Sussex, when an old man struck the board very loudly with his fist and cried 'Golier', at which the rest broke out in chorus:

> And I will sing Golier!
> Golier, Golier, Golier, Golier,
> And I will sing Golier!

which, he adds, was the whole of the poem.

Arthur Beckett is certainly an informant we can depend on, and in the 'Spirit of the Downs' he writes: 'Many were the sets of words fitted to the popular air "Lilliburlero". Among them was the toast known as "There was an old Woman":

> There was an old woman drawn up in a basket
> Three or four times as high as the moon;
> And where she was going I never did ask it,
> But in her hand she carried a broom.
> A broom! a broom! a broom! a broom
> That grows on yonder hill,
> And blows with a yellow blossom,
> Just like a lemon peel,
> Just like lemon peel, my boys,
> To mix with our English beer;
> And you shall drink it all up
> While we do say, Goliere.
> Goliere! Goliere! Goliere! Goliere!

> While we do say, Goliere!
> And you shall drink it all up
> While we do say Goliere!

This doesn't help very much, really. In fact, it tends to obscure and confuse the issue and we are left as much in the dark as ever. Why should this song, which was sung widely up to the first decade of this century, disappear so completely while so many of its contemporaries have survived? In all my experience in meeting and recording singers of traditional Sussex songs I have never met anyone who has even heard of it.

'BREKFUST!' The unmistakable voice of Gordon caused the bedroom door to rattle and brought me up with a start. 'Coming,' I answered rather feebly. The meal over, I sipped my coffee and said, 'There's no better start to a day than a good breakfast. It sets a man up and augurs well for the day ahead.'

I asked Gordon if he could throw any light on the Golier song and he told me that 'goliarding' was the term used for a form of improvisation in songs in which individual singers add extemporary verses to a song as it proceeds. He remembered that this was quite often done at his family's singsongs. He also thought the word must bear some relation to the 'golierdys', a class of educated jesters, buffoons and authors of satirical Latin verse who flourished in Germany, France and England in the twelfth and thirteenth centuries. A great deal of this work, he added, is questionably attributed to Walter Map of that period, who was one of the principal creators of the Round Table legends. It was the poetry of Bohemian life and of the tavern, written by students who had quit the universities and taken to the road, showing no regard for authority. They were disciples of the fictional character Golias, a kind of medieval Lord of Misrule – a jovial railer, greedy, drunken, licentious and witty – and their work has been described as trivial, amorous, scurrilous and coarse.

Fascinating as all of this was, we had got no nearer to the actual song that Belloc talks about, and Gordon himself had never heard of it.

If the full appreciation of a walk such as this depends to a large extent on the mood of the walker, then the kindness and companionship of my overnight hosts gave me a splendid send-off that morning and I took to the road in fine fettle. The songs we had sung the night before were still rattling round in my head, and I strode down the road away from Pease Pottage with a song, or rather a number of songs, in my heart if not actually on my lips. From time to time, through sheer exuberance, a well-known chorus would well up irresistibly and make itself heard on the morning air. I doubt if there were any human ears near enough to hear it, but it matters not, for the joy of a song is in the singing. There is nothing in life quite so uplifting as giving voice to a favourite tune when out in the open countryside, and it is an excellent way of giving thanks for the fact that you are alive and well, and striding over God's good earth under a kindly heaven.

That Belloc was happy hereabouts we have not the slightest doubt. Back in Tilgate Forest he had said, 'Now the woods smell of home', and one senses that from then on the walk took on an intimate and more affectionate aspect.

For my part I was just entering that part of the county that Belloc had known for so long and loved so well, and which had inspired some of his finest and warmest writings. As a small boy in 1878 he had come with his widowed mother

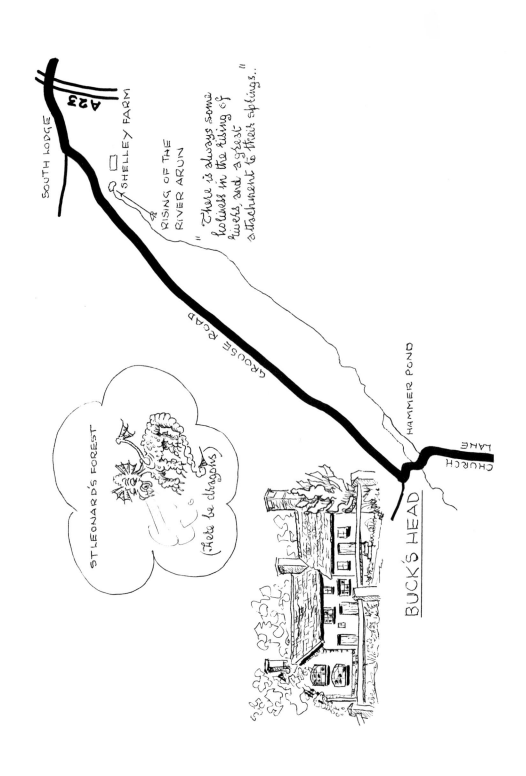

SOUTH LODGE

A23

SHELLEY FARM

RISING OF THE RIVER ARUN

"There is always some holiness in the rising of rivers, and a great attachment to their springs."

GROUSE ROAD

ST LEONARD'S FOREST

(Here be dragons)

HAMMER POND

CHURCH LANE

BUCK'S HEAD

to live in Slindon, and his love affair with Sussex started almost at once. In an essay 'The Mowing of a Field' he wrote:

> In this place, when I was a boy, I pushed through a fringe of beeches that made a complete screen between me and the world, and I came to a glade called No Man's Land. I climbed beyond it, and I was surprised and glad, because from the ridge of that glade I saw the sea.

Seventy-five years later he ended his days at King's Land, Shipley, a mere fourteen miles away, where he had lived since 1906. This rambling maze of a building, full of corridors, rooms and hallways, which had once been the village shop, was his home for nearly fifty years. Here he entertained the great and good of the parliamentary and literary worlds he inhabited when in the capital, and here he wrote much of his best work.

The magic of this part of West Sussex took him by the heart with a tender but powerful grip, and never once let go:

> Lift up your hearts in Gumber, laugh the Weald
> And you my mother the Valley of Arun sing.
> Here am I homeward from my wandering,
> Here am I homeward and my heart is healed.

It was this sense of peace and homecoming that seemed most deeply to affect him, and the river Arun stood at the centre of his devotions.

I turned down into Grouse Road, for this is the way my illustrious predecessors had gone. Bearing in mind Belloc's love of the Arun, I took a lane to the left leading to Shelley Farm. There, a little way along, I came to a quite small pond surrounded by willows and young ash trees, and I knew this to be one of the headwaters of that river. There was a margin of reeds around its edges, and a flotilla of mallards cruising in the open water sent a chevron of corrugations across the placid surface. It was a tranquil scene. 'There is always some holiness in the rising of rivers,' the Poet had said, 'and a great attachment to their springs.'

I crossed the lane and looked down through the tangled undergrowth to where I could hear, but not see, the waters trickling away southward between the fields of stubble, to where it would eventually flow into Hammer Pond, as we shall discover.

The road is a long one, a little over three miles in all, and at various high points there are splendid views of the South Downs, 'a day's march away to the south'. Unfortunately, probably because of the increased density of the woodlands, I failed to gain a viewpoint where the entire range of hills from Wolstonbury through to Duncton could be seen in one panoramic prospect such as Grizzlebeard described:

> I see before me the Weald in a tumbled garden, Wolstonbury above New Timber and Highden and Rackham beyond. . . . and far away westward I see under Duncton the Garden of Eden, I think, to which we are bound. And sitting crowned in the middle place I see Chanctonbury, which, I think, a dying man remembers so fixed against the south, if he is a man from Ashurst, or from Thakeham, or from the pine-woods by the rock, whenever by some evil fortune a Sussex man dies far away from home.

At Buck's Head I turned left, and though the road had been falling steadily for the last mile or so, here it dropped even more sharply and curved round by Hammer Pond Guest House. This is a pretty building with a Horsham stone roof and brick and white weather-boarded walls, standing under the trees below the level of the road, with a beech hedge around and a copper beech in the garden. On the opposite side is Hammer Pond, a large expanse of water. '. . . that long lake you see with a lonely wood about either shore,' Myself had said, 'is the place where Arun rises'.

About fifty yards farther on is a little brick bridge under which the water from the lake cataracts down into a deep pool at the bottom of a fern-clad ghyll: 'By this time we had come to the lake foot, where a barrier holds in the water, and the road crosses upon a dam. And we watched as we passed it the plunge of the cascade.'

I walked on, the road climbing as steeply on this side of the bridge as it falls on the other, and turned right into Church Lane, then down along past Plummer's Plain to Docker's Lodge on the A279. Turning right towards Horsham I was glad of the comfort and convenience of a footpath, for the road is busy and fast-moving. I followed the path bearing left at The Plough Inn into Leechpond Hill and so down to Crabtree.

It is difficult to decide exactly where the Sailor, who was obviously in a singing mood, burst loudly and joyfully into song while his three confederates swelled the choruses, but it was somewhere just before they reached Crabtree:

> On Sussex hills where I was bred,
> When lanes in autumn rains are red,
> When Arun tumbles in his bed,
> And busy great gusts go by;
> When branch is bare in Burton Glen
> And Bury Hill is whitening, then,
> I drink strong ale with gentlemen;
> Which nobody can deny, deny,
> Deny, deny, deny, deny,
> Which nobody can deny!

(For full version see p. 124)

> . . . the Sailor said, 'Now, was that not a good song?' 'Yes,' said I, 'and well suited to this morning and to this air, and to that broad sight of the lower land which now spreads out before us.' For even as I spoke we had come to that little shelf on which the Crabtree stands, and from which one may see the Downs all stretched before one, and Bramber Gap, and in the notch of it the high roof of Lancing; and then onwards, much further away, Arundel Gap and the hills and woods of home. It was certainly in the land beneath us, and along the Weald, which we overlooked, that once, many years ago, a young man must have written this song.

And he of all people should have known. He wrote it, of course.

Belloc would not recognize The Crabtree Inn today with its neo-Georgian façade; and the Sailor would most certainly fail to make his song heard above the din of passing traffic. But here it was that they sat outside drinking ale, and eating

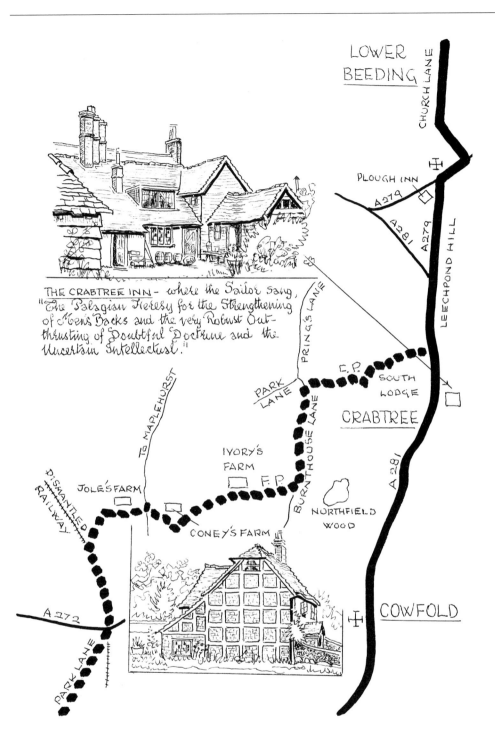

LOWER BEEDING

CHURCH LANE

PLOUGH INN

A279

A281

A279

LEECHPOND HILL

THE CRABTREE INN – where the Sailor sang,
"The Pelagian Heresy for the Strengthening
of Men's Backs and the very Robust Out-
thrusting of Doubtful Doctrine and the
Uncertain Intellectual."

PRING'S LANE

F.P.

PARK LANE

SOUTH LODGE

CRABTREE

TO MAPLEHURST

BURNTHOUSE LANE

IVORY'S FARM

F.P.

A281

JOLE'S FARM

DISMANTLED RAILWAY

CONEY'S FARM

NORTHFIELD WOOD

A272

COWFOLD

PARK LANE

bread and cheese while they discussed the occasions when and locations where it was still possible for a man to sing in a public place without attracting the attention of the police. Grizzlebeard had wondered if it would be permissible to sing there at The Crabtree Inn, but Myself thought not: 'Not outside, nor at this hour,' he had said. But the Sailor was willing to make the experiment and heartily launched into the 'Song of the Pelagian Heresy for the Strengthening of Men's Backs and the very Robust Out-thrusting of Doubtful Doctrine and the Uncertain Intellectual':

> Pelagius lived in Kardanoel,
> And taught a doctrine there,
> How whether you went to Heaven or Hell,
> It was your own affair.
> How, whether you found eternal joy
> Or sank forever to burn,
> It had nothing to do with the Church, my boy,
> But was your own concern.

(For full version see p. 125)

His song, which Grizzlebeard had called blasphemous, attracted an audience of 'half the inhabitants of that hill', and he went on to address them in rather

The Crabtree Inn outside which the Sailor sang the 'Pelagian Heresy'

high-flown language, which some of them might have found difficult to comprehend. But he also left five shillings on the table against which they were invited 'to order ale to breaking point', which they all understood perfectly, and our travellers strode down the road to the sound of cheering.

If their presence at Crabtree had caused a great stir in the village, my appearance on the scene that autumn morning occurred without remark. Inside the inn I was the only occupant of the bar, probably because it still wanted an hour to noon, but the young woman behind the counter was pleasant enough and she served my pint of bitter with a smile. Presently I confided to her the significance of my visit and pointed out the relevant parts in *the book*, and she appeared to be duly impressed. But when, in a suitably modulated voice, I sang the Sailor's song her facial expressions changed progressively as the song proceeded. She was, at first, quite intrigued; then bewildered; then completely baffled; and finally, convinced that she had a lunatic on her hands, charmingly tolerant and a little embarrassed. But the deed had been done. I had fulfilled a long-standing ambition and I felt better for it. I ordered another drink and one for her for her kindness.

I then considered the prospect of walking the long road to Ashurst via Cowfold and Henfield, which the Four Men had taken originally, and which, in 1950, I had also followed with no intolerable inconvenience from passing traffic. But the road is that much busier now, the cars faster, and with very little in the way of footpaths at the roadside the outlook was not inviting. I took the map from my haversack and, after a short perusal, the answer came to me. For the sake of an extra three or four miles I could detour to the west and arrive at Ashurst via West Grinstead and Shipley where, at King's Land, Belloc had lived for the greater part of his life. I could also look at his windmill and visit his final resting place at West Grinstead RC church. I plotted a course following footpaths, bridleways and lanes that would lead me there by the quietest possible route.

Before taking to the road I walked round the back where the tiled gables and brick chimney-stacks of the old building remained unaltered and the view to the south across the lower lands of the Weald did more than justice to Myself's description.

Retracing my steps up the A281 for about 300 yards I took a well-posted Public Bridleway into the woods immediately to the north of South Lodge Hotel and Restaurant. Down through the wood I went in a south-westerly direction on a path that was quite defined, although in places it threaded its way through thick undergrowth of waist-high bracken. Rabbits gambolling in the open spaces scampered off at my approach.

A finger-post indicated where the footpath left the bridleway, turned right down a little dip and over a stream on a simple plank bridge, to cross open country and emerge into Burnthouse Lane, just to the east of its junction with Park Lane and Pring's Lane. Following the lane southward for about three-quarters of a mile I turned westward onto a footpath to Ivory's Farm. Presently I came to Coney's Farm, a small picturesque sixteenth-century farmhouse in a well-tended garden, and this is where I had the good fortune to meet John, who has lived there for the last twenty-five years.

As we passed the time of day one thing led to another and he asked me in. There in the welcome cool of his living room, for the day was very hot, we sat and talked about this part of the county, which he knows very well, but not before John had disappeared down the stone steps of his cellar to return with two glasses of dark, old English, home-brewed ale. This ale was good; this ale was strong – you could almost have stood a teaspoon up in it! This ale was that which Englishmen drank before the hop had been introduced to the country in the fifteenth century. Of this ale it could be said, as John Nyren said of the ale at Hambledon:

> Not the modern horror under the same name, that drives as many men melancholy-mad as the hypocrites do; – not the beastliness of these days that will make a fellows inside like a shaking bog, and as rotten; but barley corn such as would put the souls of three butchers into one weaver. Ale that would flare like turpentine – genuine Boniface!

We sat there in front of a large inglenook fireplace, on the hearth of which stood a large spray of late summer flowers, drinking the ale while John told me much that was new to me about these parts in general, and in particular about West Grinstead where he was born. I am not quite sure how Belloc's name cropped up, but it did, and John told me that, as a boy, he used to work for Belloc in the garden at King's Land, and was paid one shilling (5p) for his Saturday morning's work. He now cherishes the memory that, on Belloc's eightieth birthday in 1950, he was called indoors with another boy who was working there and presented to the great man. They were given a slice of cake each and a glass of lemonade for the occasion, but what most impressed young John was the large wart on Belloc's right cheek. Memory fixes on such extraordinary details.

First-hand Bellocian stories on the verge of becoming legends abound in this neighbourhood. I heard of how he used to rush into the barber's shop at Nuthurst for a haircut and always seemed to be in a great hurry, dashing first into and then out of the shop with his cloak flying out behind him in the wind caused by his haste. I recalled the story told to me by the Reverend Ronald, whom I once met at Sutton, through which our walk will take us in due course. The gentleman had at one time been the incumbent at Shipley, and while there he got to know Peter, the son of the miller who had worked Belloc's mill there. When Peter was a boy he was playing one day outside King's Land close to the mill, when Belloc came to the door of the house and hailed him. 'You, boy, come here!' he called, crooking his finger. 'Do you play cards?'

'Yes, sir – please, sir,' came the diffident reply.

'Do you play bridge?'

'No, sir.'

'What *do* you play, boy?'

'Black Jack, sir.'

'O-oh,' growled Belloc, 'I suppose that'll do. Come along inside.'

Peter followed, cap in hand, and made up a four at cards, spending the rest of the afternoon playing Black Jack in the company of Belloc, G.K. Chesterton and Sir (then Mr) Winston Churchill.

Another story from the same source told how, in the early thirties, a young lady teacher travelled daily to the village school on a motor cycle, and her route took her past King's Land at about a quarter to nine every morning. This daily shattering of the profound peace and silence from which, we might assume, the great man drew much of his inspiration was too much for him. He stormed out one morning, stood four-square in the middle of the road and prevented her passing. 'If you must go to your school by this road,' he thundered, 'get off that wretched thing, switch off the engine and walk past my house. If you want to ride it, you will have to go the long way round.' Henceforth, I was told, the hapless young lady adopted the second suggestion.

While we had been swapping tales John had placed on the table large helpings of bread and cheese, and he then offered to accompany me to Shipley to show me the way. Soon after, with his dog, Sadie, trotting obediently to heel, we set off up the road a little way to Jole's Farm, where we turned left onto a footpath that took us to the dismantled railway down which we walked until we came to Park Lane. To the west of the lane is West Grinstead Park, and John pointed across to where stood Pope's Oak, the tree under which, in the early eighteenth century, Alexander Pope is reputed to have written 'The Rape of the Lock'.

At the bottom of Park Lane we came to West Grinstead Roman Catholic Church and turned into the churchyard, where to the east of the church we found Belloc's grave. Above the grave is an oaken memorial headboard recording the deaths in the family: his son Peter, a captain in the Royal Marines, who died on active service on 2 April 1941; Elodie, his wife, who died on 2 February 1914; and, finally, his own:

Belloc's grave

> Also of her husband Hilaire Belloc on the feast of Our Lady of Mount Carmel, 16th. July, 1953. Aged 83 years. "I go to prepare a place for you, I will come again and will take you to myself, that where I am you may also be."

On the outside wall to the right of the door as you go in through the eastern entrance to the church is a stone tablet inscribed:

> Five yards east of this stone lies the body of Hilaire Belloc, 1870–1953. For 48 years a member of the congregation of this Church of Our Lady of Consolation, in whose memory this tower and spire were completed in 1964, in grateful recognition of his zealous & unwavering profession of our Holy Faith which he defended in his writings and noble verse. 'This is The faith that I have held and hold and This is That in which I mean to die.'

A short way to the right along the B2135 we turned south where a signpost indicated 'Parish Church', and passed the rectory where half a dozen Aylesbury ducks adorned the lawn by a small pond. About eight miles away we could see the long, low line of the South Downs from Truleigh Hill all along westward past Chanctonbury, still emaciated from the hurricane. John pointed out the large and ancient houses that speak of the prosperity of West Grinstead in the days before the river silted up. William de Braose of Bramber Castle had been awarded the Rape of Bramber, in which all this part of the county is situated, for services to Duke William in the Battle of Hastings. He built the original Knepp Castle, of which only a ruined fragment remains, as a stronghold, but would sometimes sail up the river with his retinue and use it as a hunting lodge. The river in those days was the main means of transport and communication between West Grinstead

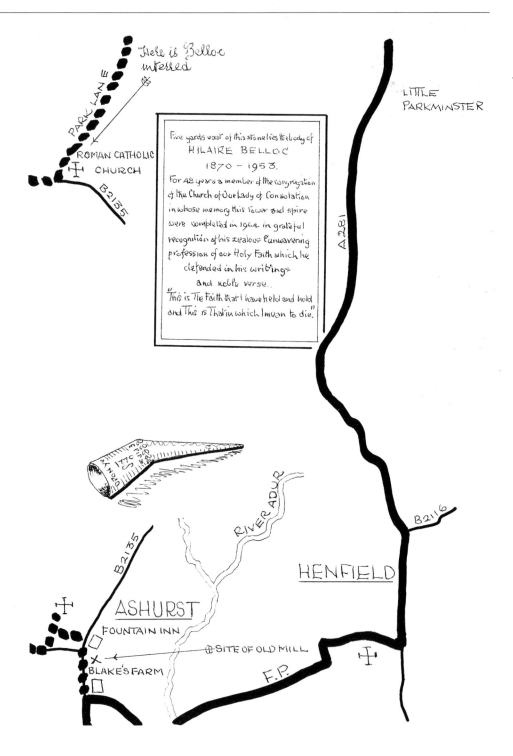

Here is Belloc
interred

PARK LANE

ROMAN CATHOLIC
CHURCH

B2135

Five yards east of this stone lies the body of
HILAIRE BELLOC
1870 – 1953.
For 48 years a member of the congregation
of the Church of Our Lady of Consolation
in whose memory this tower and spire
were completed in 1964 in grateful
recognition of his zealous & unwavering
profession of our Holy Faith which he
defended in his writings
and noble verse.
"This is The Faith that I have held and hold
and This is That in which I mean to die."

LITTLE
PARKMINSTER

A281

B2116

RIVER ADUR

B2135

HENFIELD

ASHURST
FOUNTAIN INN
⊕ SITE OF OLD MILL
X
BLAKE'S FARM
F.P.

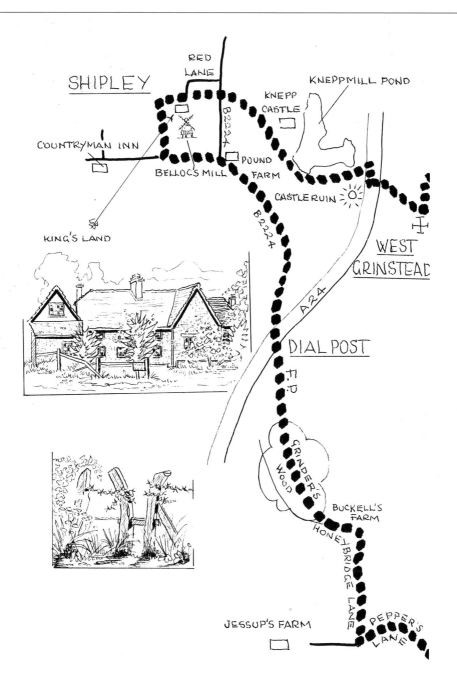

SHIPLEY

RED LANE

KNEPPMILL POND

KNEPP CASTLE

B2224

COUNTRYMAN INN

POUND FARM

BELLOC'S MILL

CASTLE RUIN

KING'S LAND

B2224

WEST GRINSTEAD

A24

DIAL POST

F.P.

GRINDER'S WOOD

BUCKELL'S FARM

HONEYBRIDGE LANE

JESSUP'S FARM

PEPPER'S LANE

and Bramber, which was then a seaport and, as such, an important link with the Continent, and this prosperity continued all the time the river was navigable. However, when the river silted up West Grinstead's fortunes receded with the water, and it was left to become a rather isolated and straggling hamlet in the fields, albeit graced by some handsome houses. Glebe House is one of those beautiful old houses, with a pond fringed by bulrushes and a large commodious oak tree on the green beside.

We reached the twelfth-century church of St George, with its fifteenth-century wooden porch, and inside paused to look at the ancient oaken pews, which bear the names of farms and holdings in the district. Ivory's, Coney's and Jole's we have already met, but there were many more, such as Swallow's Nest, Rooklands, Pinland, Highlands, Clothets, Sands, Prior's Bine and Thistlewell – names that read like a medieval area directory.

We returned to the path and went on towards the A24, which we joined just above the ruined remains of old Knepp Castle – but not for long. We turned onto a footpath through Knepp Castle Estate, which took us past the foot of Knepp Lake, or Kneppmill Pond, which feeds the river Adur. This is one of the largest lakes in Sussex, with trees that run down to the shores on either side and a distant view of stubble fields away to the north. There were lots of water birds. Offshore a dozen gleaming white swans floated as serenely as P&O liners at anchor, while mallards and moorhens fussed about in the shallows like rusty coasters.

Soon we passed the existing Knepp Castle, a noble, castellated pile over to our right, the seat of the Burrells, and then on over the B2224 into Red Lane. This in turn led us to King's Land, a rambling, brick-built house with a Horsham stone roof, and also to Shipley Windmill. Belloc's ghost still walks these high-hedged lanes – that bulky, dark-clad figure in the flowing cloak is for ever just around the next corner, and his deathless utterances are on the breeze:

> He does not die that can bequeath
> Some influence to the land he knows,
> Or dares, persistent, interwreath
> Love permanent with the wild hedgerows;
> He does not die, but still remains
> Substantiate with his darling plains.

I stood on the millstone doorstep of the mill and read the inscription over the door: 'Let this be a memorial to Hilaire Belloc who garnered a harvest of wisdom and sympathy for young and old – MDCCCLXX–MCMLIII [1870–1953].' And below that: 'The best known smock mill in West Sussex built in 1879 and restored by the County Council as a memorial to the writer Hilaire Belloc who lived nearby.' In the mill field is also a well-head with a wooden windlass protected by a small roof of thatch.

Leaving the mill we passed on down the path, which was paved spasmodically with large tabular slabs of Horsham stone, and over the duck-weeded river Adur by a wooden footbridge. We came to a lane onto which we turned west, and this led to the Countryman Inn, a welcome sight with its friendly sign. In fact it was an altogether pleasant and attractive building, standing quite alone with twin gables at each end, chimneys atop, a twin-gabled porch over the front door and

King's Land, Shipley, near Horsham, the home of Hilaire Belloc from 1906 until the time of his death in 1953

window-boxes on both storeys ablaze with colour. The door was open, a sight that cheered the hearts of two walking men that day. Here we were to meet John's charming wife who would convey him home by car. His pleasant company and informative chat had enriched my day.

I walked back along the road to Pound Corner with wide views across fields of stubble on either side. To the north were Belloc's windmill and Shipley church, and southward the Downs and Chanctonbury Ring. At Pound Corner I took the road to Dial Post.

On my own again I swung down the lane and, knowing that I had at least six miles ahead of me, stepped out strongly. The way was pleasant and the September evening was golden and warm. It was also quiet, and the number of pheasants and woodpigeons foraging at the laneside told me that few cars used this road. Apart from the tarmacadam surface the lane could not have changed in two hundred years, and some of the trees, which in places met overhead, must have been there for all of that time, especially the oaks.

With the unquestionable advantages that my detour had brought still uppermost in my mind, I turned my mental attention to what I might have sacrificed by abandoning the original route so blatantly. What had I missed? I would not be passing through Cowfold, but *the book* tells us that nothing of significance happened there anyway:

Shipley's windmill

When we had come to Little Cowfold, which we did very shortly, it was already past three in the afternoon, and therefore in such early weather (more winter than autumn) the air had a touch of evening, and looking at the church there and admiring it, we debated whether we would stop in that place a little while and pick a quarrel with anyone, or lacking that, sing another song, or lacking that, drink silently. For Virgil says, '*Propria quae Cowfold Carmen Cervisia Ludus*'.

But it was so late we thought we would not do any of these things but take the way along to Henfield and get us near to the Downs, though how far we should go that night we none of us could tell.

But I should also miss Henfield, and Henfield was a different matter:

And so when it was full dark we came to Henfield, and determined that it was time for bread, and for bacon, and for ale – a night meal inspired by the road and by the tang of the cold. For you must know that once again, though it was yet so early in the year, a very slight frost had nipped the ground.

We made therefore for the inn in that place, and asked the mistress of it to fry us bacon, and with it to give us bread and as much ale as four men could drink by her judgment and our own.

Here it was – although it is not clear at which particular inn – they talked about how 'Hog is made so suitable for Man', and, after Myself had given a protracted dissertation on the curing of ham, in which he touched on the fact that 'the pig, like all brutes, differs from man in this, that his hide is covered with hair', he burst into song:

> The dog is a faithful, intelligent friend,
> But his hide is covered with hair;
> The cat will inhabit the house to the end,
> But *her* hide is covered with hair.

(For full version see p. 127)

But Grizzlebeard had cut him short with, 'Enough! Enough! These songs, which rival the sea-serpent in length, are no part of the true poetic spirit.'

As I went my way that evening I sang the song at the top of my voice to the annoyance, certainly, of no one in this world; and, I hope, without too much disapproval from anyone in the next who knows it better than I.

In due course the four had left the inn at Henfield, traversed the water-meadows and crossed a wooden bridge over the river Adur to Ashurst. As I hoped to be in Ashurst well before dark I concluded that the alternative route I had taken, and which added so much Bellocian flavour to the walk, was well worth whatever extra effort had been required and what minor sacrifices necessary.

I came to Dial Post and the old A24 close to the Crown Inn and took a footpath to the north of and hard by the inn, which took me over the busy new A24 and across the fields. Just before I got to Grinder's Wood I put up a flock of ten or a dozen goldfinches that had been feeding on a patch of thistles run to seed, and their red, black and white hoods and the streak of gold in their wings went

Henfield, c. 1900, where at the inn Myself told how 'Hog was made so suitable to Man'

flashing away in the evening sunlight. I emerged from Grinder's Wood over a stile into Honeybridge Lane, just west of a house called The Firs.

After an acute-angled turn to the left about a mile farther on, the lane becomes Pepper's Lane. This would have led me directly into Ashurst, but, as I was in good time, I turned up Church Lane and visited the church with its short, square tower, shingled spire and roofs of Horsham slabs. Dedicated to St James, the earliest part having been built in the late twelfth century, this church is thoroughly charming. What remains in my memory very clearly is the eighteenth-century vamping horn displayed over a doorway in the north wall, one of only eight known to be in the country. It is said to be the smallest at three feet in length including the sounding bell, which opens to seven inches in diameter, set at an angle to the main body of the horn and mouthpiece. The painted inscription is still clearly visible: 'Praise Him Upon ye Strings & Pipe. Palmer fecit. 1770.' It must have provided an impressive, if crude, accompaniment to the psalms and hymns of the choir and might even, one is tempted to think, have given John Fuller's twelve trombones a run for their money.

I took a path eastward just to the south of the church that led me directly to the inn, that other bastion of English village life, which, together with the church, over the years has provided the twin-pillared support of rural harmony and spiritual well-being. This was the Fountain Inn at Ashurst where the Sailor came for ale. But let us, as they say, get over the stile one leg at a time.

Fountain Inn, Ashurst

Standing back from the road the inn remains substantially the same as it was at the turn of the century. The only detectable difference when compared with a fading sepia photograph on the wall inside, which was taken at about that time, is the porch over the front door. Indoors the bar and its furnishings have been similarly preserved and now look pretty much the same, one imagines, as when the Sailor came here with 'a great two-gallon can and soon returned with it full of Steyning ale'.

I sat there in a comfortable kitchen carver under the heavily timbered ceiling with my boots stretched out before me on the flagstone floor and absorbed the scene, and likewise a very welcome pint of bitter beer. Almost the whole of one side of the small room was taken up by a huge, wide-mouthed inglenook fireplace with an immense oak lintel, and two wooden benches on the hearth on which four men, two on either side, could sit and toast their toes on winter evenings. Tonight, of course, there was no fire, but there was no loss of dignity for the lack of it. The neat mound of ash with brushwood and logs on top awaited, like a faithful servant, the first call to service when frost threatened, with warmth, comfort and cheer when required.

The other three occupants of the bar sat on hardwood kitchen chairs at cross-legged trestle tables, indulging that time-honoured English custom of sipping ale over desultory verbal exchanges at the close of day. A clock-ticking calm prevailed.

The day was beginning to catch up with me. I had walked a good fifteen miles and a certain weariness was setting in, but as the level of the golden life-giver in my glass lowered, sup by sup, my spirits gradually revived.

The landlord, Maurice, proved to be a very friendly sort of chap. He took an interest in the walk I was on because he had read *the book* and therefore already knew of the Sailor's visit to the inn. He also had some invaluable information to impart. He told me that the generally accepted opinion among the local people, whose collective knowledge of the locality goes back for several generations, was that 'the little house' in Ashurst, in which the Four Men had spent the night, was Bergen-op-Zoom, a tiny building about three-quarters of a mile south of the inn on the east side of the B2135.

This exciting new evidence brought the original walk back again sharply into focus, and I could not wait to see the place. But before I left, and with Maurice's help, I consulted both *the book* and the map, and was delighted to find that Bergen-op-Zoom was clearly marked on the map by name. Then I walked off down the road as fast as my legs would carry me, and as I walked I theorized that, if they had crossed the river at Bineham's Bridge and followed the footpath until it came out on the road at Blake's Farm, from there they could quite easily have seen the windmill that was there in those days.

So we went over the water-meadows. It was very cold, and the moon rode over Chanctonbury in a clear heaven. We did not speak. We plodded on all four, in single file, myself leading, along the narrow path by the bare hedge-side. The frost had touched the grass, and the twigs of quickset were sharp in the moonlight like things engraved upon metal. We came out upon the Ashurst road. The mill was all sound in those days, and the arms of it stood against the sky. We walked abreast, but still in silence: the Poet slouched and Grizzlebeard let his stick trail along the ground, and even the Sailor had a melancholy air, though his strong legs carried him well. As for me I still pressed onwards a little ahead of the line, for I knew my goal near at hand, while for my three companions it was but an aimless trudge through the darkness after a long day's journey. So did we near that little house which God knows I love as well as any six or seven little houses in the world.

So far, so good. I passed Blake's Farm where they would have turned south onto the road, and my mind's eye could see the four figures ahead of me as Belloc had described them.

We came to the foot of a short hill: tall elms stood out against the sky a short way back from the road and beyond a little green. Beneath them shone the thatch of a vast barn, and next it a sight which I knew very well. . . . the roof and chimney.

I, too, came to the foot of a short hill. It was not much of a hill as hills go, mind you. I had travelled this road before by car and not even noticed it, but if you are travelling on foot there is a quite noticeable upward gradient and, as it fitted the theory, I seized on the fact eagerly. There were also trees against the sky – not elms, of course, for the late lamented elm tree is a thing of the past here since the devastation of Dutch Elm disease. There were oaks and other trees, and a sizeable green, which runs down in front of New Wharf Farm. There were also latter-day barns and outbuildings of precast concrete and asbestos but not, alas, any sign of the 'thatch of a vast barn', which, after the passage of nearly ninety years, would have been asking rather a lot, I suppose.

Then to my delight, just discernible through the green cover over to my left, I spotted the tiled roof and red-brick chimney of Bergen-op-Zoom. I crossed the road and was looking over the gate into the garden when a man approached from the house and, before I had a chance to greet him, he addressed me by name. Then I recognized him. It was Michael, an accomplished and popular fiddle-player of the old school, and a familiar sight and sound at Folk Festivals and the like up and down the country. We had already met several times at different places where folk music is played and traditional songs are sung.

Bergen-op-Zoom

He invited me indoors and I was introduced to his nonagenerian father, who had served in the Royal Flying Corps (The Cavalry of the Clouds) during the First World War, and they both made me very welcome. Neither was aware of Belloc's reputed connection with their home, but after I had told them that in the collective folk memory of the village the Four Men had spent the night under that roof, and backed up the claim by reading relevant passages from *the book*, they were as convinced as I that it was true.

I took from my pocket a great key, and when my companions saw this their merriment returned to them, for they knew that I had found the shelter. . . . I turned the key in the lock, and there, within, when I had struck a match, appeared the familiar room. The beam of the ceiling was a friend to me and the great down-fire-place inhabited the room. There, in that recess, lay on the dogs and the good pile of ashes, a faggot and four or five huge logs of cord wood, of oak from the clay of the Weald: I lit beneath all these a sheaf of verse I had carried about for months, but which had disappointed me, and the flames leapt up, in shape like leaves of holly. It was a good sight to see.

As I sat there reading this aloud I could see 'the beam of the ceiling' that was a friend to him over my head, and the 'great down-fire-place' that inhabited the room before me, but in the recess, instead of the faggot and logs on the pile of ash there was a cast-iron wood-burning stove, two wheel-back chairs and a copper warming-pan hanging on the back wall. It was still a good sight to see and I feel quite certain that it was here that

With the fire humanity returned; we talked, we spread our hands; one pulled the curtains over the long low window of the room, another brought the benches near the blaze, benches with high backs and dark with age; another put the boards on the trestles before it; another lit two candles and stood them in their own grease upon the boards. We were in a new mood, being come out of the night and seeing the merriment of the fire.
Next we would send to the Fountain for drink. For the inn of Ashurst is called the Fountain Inn. It is not the Fountain called the 'Fount of Gold' of which it is written –

This is that water from the Fount of Gold
Water of youth and washer out of cares.

The Fountain of Ashurst runs, by God's grace, with better stuff than water.

Precisely as I had discovered to my great joy less than an hour before. The little cameo seemed complete and an important piece of the jigsaw had fallen into place.
I asked Michael how the house had come by its peculiar name. He replied:

Sometime before 1800 it was thought to be a good thing to improve the navigation on the river Adur and New Wharf Farm, which is the next farm down. This is still called Malthouse Lane so I guess there was a malthouse at the end of it, and they wanted to bring the barley up and down the river in barges for the maltings.
So, anyway, to improve the river a navigational engineer was brought over from Holland to supervise the work that was necessary, and while he worked on the river they built him this small house to live in. His native village in Holland was Bergen-op-Zoom and he named the house after the village; and nobody has ever troubled to change it.

I had booked in for the night at the hotel at Nash's Farm, so I had about a mile and half to walk, and the last stage of my day's journey was to be over the same path as the Four Men had taken on the morning following their stay at Bergen-op-Zoom.

So we went out through the door and across the little green to a wobble road that is there, and by a way across the fields to Steyning, where we should find the high road to Washington and Storrington and Amberley Bridge, and so over to the country beyond Arun and the things we knew.

I bade farewell to Michael and his father and crossed the green in front of New Wharf Farm, turning left at the bottom of it into the 'little wobble road that is there', which leads to Upper Northover Farm. It is signposted 'Public Bridleway'.

At Upper Northover Farm I turned right and down through Heron Farm, where the footpath, over stiles, is plainly posted. I passed a patch of chicory in full bloom, with its daisy-like blossoms of that exquisite shade of pale blue found in the hedge sparrow's egg, or sometimes in evening skies. There were still quite a lot of flowers to be seen: the fleabane's shining gold in the field margins; the brindled purple of the Indian balsam in the dried out ditches; and the ubiquitous convolvulus tangling up into the hedgerows to lend its pale-pink bells to the shorn and withering hawthorn; but the wild clematis was beginning to change from the green of traveller's joy into the fluffy seed heads of old man's beard; and the seeding cuckoo pints were assuming their scarlet mantles that would elevate them to lords and ladies. The pageantry of summer was merging into the fecundity of autumn.

Though well indicated by fingerposts, the path is, in places, overgrown and obviously seldom used, but all the time the line of the Downs draws closer and looms larger, with Chanctonbury's mutilated crown always away to the south-west.

The light was still strong in the sky, but the softer hues of evening were becoming apparent and a faint mist was forming at ground level as the sun sank over Parham. There prevailed that deep inland peace that falls about the countryside in late evening when the shades of night begin to blur the familiar outlines of our daytime world. Here, away from the affairs of men, all but the nocturnal creatures were seeking shelter and sleep, and a reverent silence was descending on the earth like the calm of vespers.

Although Belloc had seen it at an earlier hour in the day because the year had been more advanced, I was seeing the Adur valley much as he had as they approached Henfield, and responded to its beauty with awe.

The sky was already of an apple green to the westward, and in the eastern blue there were stars. There also shone what had not yet appeared upon that windless day, a few small wintry clouds, neat and defined in heaven. Above them the moon, past her first quarter but not yet full, was no longer pale, but began to make a cold glory; and all that valley of Adur was a great and solemn sight to see as we went forward upon our adventure that led nowhere and away. To us four men, no one of whom could know the other, and had met by I could not tell what chance, and would part very soon for ever, these things were given. All four of us together received the sacrament of that wide and silent beauty, and we ourselves went in silence to receive it.

The footpath brought me to a track that led westward to Huddlestone Farm, but I stuck to the path, which would eventually have taken me to Wyckham Farm. About 150 yards farther on, however, I left it and climbed a stile on my right, and took the path at the side of an uncut field of barley down toward Natt's Cottages, the tiled roofs and brick chimneys of which I could see rising out of the trees that surrounded them. One small, solitary window looked out from a northern wall of the farm, but no one saw my approach. It looked utterly deserted and not a little forlorn, with the rafters of an outbuilding exposed through missing tiles like the ribs of an abandoned carcass.

Over a little stream on a plank bridge I turned west and a couple of wood pigeons went clattering up through the branches of an oak as I passed to the south of the cottages; otherwise all was still. Skirting a field of bean stubble I turned south again and passed east of and close to Nash Farm, my objective, but there was no way through. So I walked round the farm to the south and, keeping to the edge of a stubble field, left the path rejoining the B2135 at its right-angle turn to the west. By the time I reached Nash Farm and the hotel it was quite dark.

Before going to rest in the 'little house' that night, Belloc had gone outside:

So I slipped to the door very quietly, covering the latch with my fingers to dumb its noise, and I went out and watched the world.

The moon stood over Chanctonbury, so removed and cold that you might almost have thought her careless of the follies of men; little clouds, her attendants, shone beneath her worshipping, and they presided together over a general silence. Her light caught the edges of the Downs. There was no mist. She was still frosty-clear when I saw her set behind those hills. The stars were more brilliant after her setting, and deep quiet held the valley of Adur, my little river, slipping at low tide towards the sea.

Later I looked out of a westward window. The night was warm and the mists had evaporated. The sky was glowing with diffused light from a brilliant moon, which itself was out of my field of vision to the south of the house. But over Chanctonbury, which stood out in a sharp silhouette, Jupiter hung poised low in the sky like a diamond pendant, watching over the sleeping world beneath. All was still – even the geese that had given me such a noisy and cautious welcome an hour or two before had dropped their guard, and the lake was silent.

Ashurst to Storrington (10 miles)

Nash Hotel has been rebuilt on the site of an ancient farmhouse and some parts of the original building, we are told, are of medieval origins. It stands in eight acres of good, fertile soil, most of which in more recent years has been turned over to viniculture and is known as the Steyning Vineyard. A more suitable spot could hardly be imagined – with its gentle southern slope in the lee of the Downs it soaks up every minute of sunshine and is protected from the prevailing winds.

The next morning I was up in good time and went outside. The day was fine with a gusty wind from the direction of the hills, bringing clusters of heavy cumulus cloud in off the sea only five miles away to the south. I strolled at a leisurely pace up between the neat, well-tended rows of vines on their wire supports, and the crop on the more mature vines looked quite splendid. A pair of peacock butterflies danced on ahead of me. They proceeded in short stages, settling a few yards in front and waiting until I had almost reached them before taking to the air and moving on again. They hadn't the wit, it seemed, to fly over

High Street, Steyning, c. 1907, with The Chequer Inn on the left and the clock-tower in the middle distance

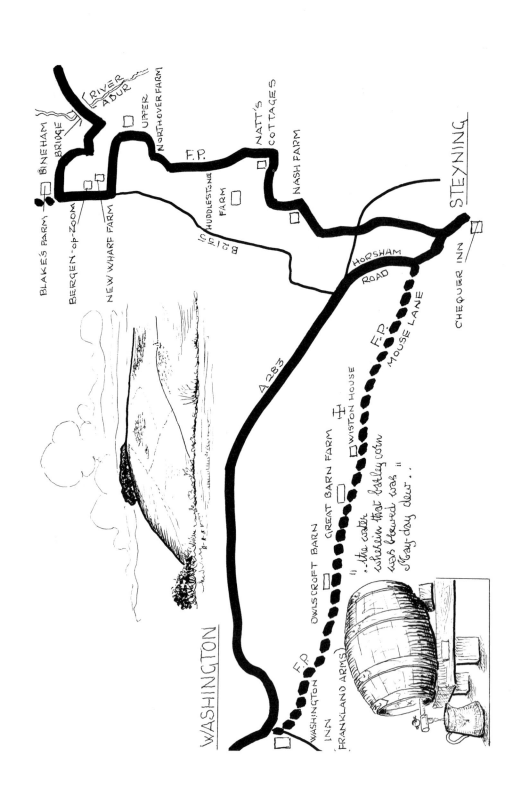

RIVER ADUR

BINEHAM BRIDGE

BLAKE'S FARM

BERGEN-op-ZOOM

NEW WHARF FARM

UPPER NORTHOVER FARM

F.P.

HUDDLESTONE FARM

B2135

NATT'S COTTAGES

NASH FARM

STEYNING

HORSHAM ROAD

CHEQUER INN

A283

MOUSE LANE

F.P.

WISTON HOUSE

GREAT BARN FARM

OWLSCROFT BARN

F.P.

WASHINGTON

WASHINGTON INN (FRANKLAND ARMS)

".. the cooler wherein that barley corn was brewed was a 'May-day clear'.."

the rows and out of my way. But then perhaps they were enjoying it and treating it as a game – there was an air of levity in their fluttering. In either case, whether witless or fun-loving, the company of a couple of butterflies on a pleasant morning in September in a flourishing vineyard was bordering on the idyllic and they put me in a happy frame of mind.

I went back into the fields and picked up the path where I had left it the previous evening, then continued south over the A283 and down into Steyning. The High Street of this pleasant little market town was alive with pedestrian shoppers, but the traffic problem has been greatly relieved by the bypass road to the north. This is one of the most attractive main streets in the county with architecture representing several centuries. If you raise your eyes above the level of the modern shop-fronts to the crooked roofs of warm, red tiles and moss-grown Horsham slabs, the brick chimneys and the walls of hung-tile or painted weatherboard, you will see what the shepherds and drovers used to see on market days, for until about seventy years ago the market was held here in the High Street. And you can still check your watch by the old clock in the little tower of the Market House.

I came to The Chequer Inn, which I have always regarded as the 'inn, hotel, guest-house, or hostelry' where the Four Men met the 'Man in the Chair' in the smoking room:

> . . . crouched up against the fire in a jolly old easy-chair, which little suited his vile and scraggy person, a being of an unpleasant sort. He had a hump which was not his fault, and a sour look which was. He was smoking a long churchwarden pipe through his sneering lips. There was very little hair upon his face, though he did not shave, and the ear turning towards us, the left ear, had been so broken that it looked pointed, and made one shudder. The sneer on his lips was completed by the long slyness of his eye. His legs were as thin as sticks, and he had one crossed over the other; his boots had elastic sides to them, and horrible tags fore and aft, and above them measly grey socks thin and wrinkled.

Chequer Inn

I went in and there indeed was a man in a chair; a man of fairly generous proportions, no longer young, with an open countenance and a frank and friendly look about him. He was in complete contrast to the man we have just read about. The spindle-back carver in which he sat so comfortably by the fireplace looked as if it might have been made to measure, or perhaps his frame had moulded itself to the chair. Probably neither, but nonetheless one felt they were made for each other.

He looked up with a grin as wide and as white as a box of peppermint creams, and I knew him at once. He had reached retirement now, but fifty years previously when we had first met as young men we had performed constabulary duties side by side on the streets of Worthing. One of the undeniable advantages of spending a lifetime in a given area is that you never know when you are going to come across an old friend. Goff, as he is known to intimates, almost leapt from the chair and greeted me like a long-lost brother in the warm, friendly accent of a West Sussex-born man, which carried more than a hint of the sound of talk in a Petworth cattle market. Over drinks we reminisced and laughed or sympathized about the way life had treated us over the fifteen or so years since last we had met.

Born in New Pound (New Pun') close to Wisborough Green, Goff, as a boy, had worked at the Unique (Unicue) Works there where they made straw-elevators for use in corn-stack building, in the days before combine harvesters. Many of the old men he worked with at that time had had their feet still well and truly planted in the last century, and he had never forgotten the peaceful, plodding tenor of their ways, the gentle tones of their dialect and their quiet, unobtrusive wit.

He reminded me of the story of the two old men leaning on a farm gate one evening. The conversation was leisurely with ten-second pipe-puffing pauses between contributions:

'Moi darter, Jane, wen' down the pictures (cinema) at Midhus' (Midhurst) laas' wik.'

'*Did* she?'

'Yeah. She sez that jest is a noice place they got down there.'

'O-aagh.'

'Yeah. She sez that's a damn sight bigger inside than 'tis out!'

We talked of the many linguistic peculiarities of the old Sussex folk. A favourite prefatory term, he told me, which was used in much the same way as we might say 'nevertheless' or 'notwithstanding', was 'let that be 'owt'll 'wiver', which is a telescoped version of 'let that be how it will, however'. They also had a habit of dropping the first syllable of a word so that 'machine', for instance, would be decapitated to ''chine'. Goff was stocking up the tool-boxes on two new elevators ready for delivery one day and in error he put two spanners in one box instead of one in each. 'No, Goff,' said his elderly workmate, 'that wun't do look. That spanner dun't 'long t' this 'chine, that 'longs t' t'other party's 'chine.'

There are two ancient adjacent farmsteads just to the west of Sayer's Common called Great Wapses and Little Wapses, and many of the older generation used that word when referring to wasps. But if you feel inclined to laugh at their ignorance, as I confess I have been tempted to do, the laugh is really on you. The word 'waeps' (pronounced wops) was the Anglo-Saxon name for that pestilent insect, and the plural was therefore 'wopsies'.

We have to bear in mind that few of these words were written down by the old people – most of them were illiterate, anyway – and we have to improvise means to convert the oral into the written to the best of our ability. This manner of adding what sounded like the suffix '–ies' to a word to produce the plural was used with words like 'ghost' and 'post', so you might hear talk of a 'row of posties'. Not content with that, some would double up on the last syllable and speak of 'ghostieses sittin' on postieses', and it is my belief that when we read about the old-timers referring to fairies as 'Pharisees' there were no biblical connotations whatever, it was merely a plural in the accepted mode, that is 'fairieses'.

Sometimes the generally accepted interpretations put on certain well-known sayings can be called into question, and occasionally 'forty thousand Frenchmen *can* be wrong'. I have mentioned elsewhere the proverb 'spoiling the sheep (ship) for a ha'p'orth of tar', and I speak as an ex-tarboy at sheep-shearing time. But my father always held that the Barley Mow, the name by which so many favourite inns are known and usually pronounced to rhyme with 'sow' as in seed, is a misnomer. It does not refer to the cutting or mowing of the barley, but to that portion of a barn in which the cut barley, or any other corn crop, is stacked prior to threshing, and is pronounced 'mow' to rhyme with sow as in pig. When that

Ploughing under Chanctonbury Ring, near Washington

end of the barn, the mow, was stacked with barley to provide malt for the October brewings it was regarded with particular affection by the threshermen and labourers who had to handle it, and that is why the barley mow is celebrated in song and so many alehouses up and down the country rejoice under the sign of the Barley Mow.

Similarly, there is a well supported opinion that 'to set the Thames on fire' should in fact read 'to set the temse on fire', referring to the sieves in a windmill. These were usually the part of a mill prone to combustion through excessive friction if in a strong wind the sails got away and revolved at a furious speed beyond the control of the miller. Windmills were almost invariably constructed of wood and, by the very nature of their function, were always tinder dry, and that is why so many windmills ended their days in flames.

Our conversation led us through a diversity of matters such as these until at last the time came for me to say goodbye to my old friend and push on westward. I walked on up the High Street past the market clock thinking how much more congenial my encounter in The Chequer Inn had been than that of my predecessors.

On the outskirts of the town, where the road takes a sharp right-hand turn into Horsham Road and so on to Washington, I entered Mouse Lane hard by an attractive, rather crooked half-timbered building, to embark on another detour. I had already given the matter considerable thought and, although Belloc is quite specific about not going through Wiston Park, 'We took the road so as not to go through Wiston Park, for though the house there is as good a sight as any in England, why, it was not ours', I had decided to do so on account of it being by far the quieter and more desirable route for anyone on foot and, in addition, there is now a public right of way through the park, which pretty obviously was not the case in 1902. Moreover, I believe it to be the original route of the old road under the hills.

Mouse Lane is a hollow way in places where the steep banks on either side are up to about 15 feet high, thickly clad with ivy and ground elder, with hazels touching fingers overhead. It compared most favourably with the endless flow of traffic I knew to exist on the A283 away to the north, the route I had rejected.

I left Mouse Lane where it takes a half-right bend through a white gate leading to Wiston House and Wilton Park, and followed the path to the south of the Tudor house, which stands shoulder to shoulder with its tiny church. This was the home of Charles Goring who, in 1760 as a young man, planted the beech saplings on the crest of the hill above his home. They grew under his carefully nurturing hand into the best-known and most affectionately regarded landmark in Sussex – Chanctonbury Ring. He lived to see it grow to maturity and, in the true spirit of the age, gave thanks to the Almighty in these lines,

> How oft around thy ring, sweet Hill,
> A Boy, I used to play,
> And form my plans to plant thy top
> On some auspicious day!
> How oft among thy broken turf
> With what delight I trod;
> With what delight I placed those twigs
> Beneath thy maiden sod!

And then an almost hopeless wish
Would creep within my breast,
Oh, could I live to see thy top
In all its beauty dressed!

That time's arrived; I've had my wish,
And lived to eighty-five;
I'll thank my God who gave such grace
As long as e'er I live.
Still when the morning sun in Spring,
Whilst I enjoy my sight,
Shall gild thy new-clothed Beech and sides,
I'll view thee with delight.

At Great Barn Farm the barn from which the farm takes its name is still splendid and elegant in old age. Well over a hundred feet long, it has a magnificent roof of local slabs, still as weather-proof as on the day it was built, while lesser and probably much younger out-buildings around it are falling into decay. I was now almost directly under Chanctonbury, although from hard under the northern slopes it could not be seen.

A little farther on the path begins to climb and wide views open out to the north and west right across toward Black Down, close on a score of miles away. Heavy, isolated rainstorms could be seen, driven by the south-westerly wind, which had freshened a good deal since early morning, although under the hills there was a certain amount of shelter. I looked across to the pine-clad Sand Rock with its armless windmill. This has long since been converted into a house and was once the home of the composer John Ireland. Though prominent and no doubt commanding an equally excellent panorama of the Downs looking south, in being deprived of its most characteristic features it has lost some of its dignity.

I walked on alongside an overgrown hedgerow where brambles were flinging their mooring lines ashore, and the path slid easily behind me. It was the fourth day out and I was gradually becoming more limber. The leisurely pace of the walker allows time for even the most ponderous of minds to perceive, absorb and adapt to the surrounding scene and a man on foot can smell the fragrance of the wayside flowers, hear the clear notes of the robin's song and experience a perfect communion with the world around him.

This was running through my mind as I went, yet Belloc, whom we know to have been one of nature's walkers with many, many long treks to his credit, wrote: 'Of the great many things which man does which he should not do or need not do, if he were wholly explained by the verb "to be", you may count walking.'

Now isn't that extraordinary? But if we read on in his incomparable essay on walking, in the Introduction to 'The Footpath Way', we detect the underlying note of humour, in whose name anything is permissible. The urge to include some of it is quite irresistible:

Just watch a man walking, if he is a proper man, and see the business of it: how he expresses his pride, or his determination, or his tenacity, or his curiosity, or perhaps his very purpose in his stride! Well, all that business of walking that you are looking at is a piece of extraordinarily skilful trick-acting, such that were the animal not known to do it you would swear he could never be trained to it by any process, however lengthy, or however minute, or however strict. This is what happens when a man walks: first of all he is in stable equilibrium, though the arc of stability is minute. If he stands with his feet well apart, his centre of gravity (which is about half way up him or a little more) may oscillate within an arc of about five degrees on either side of stability and tend to return to rest. But if it oscillates beyond that five degrees or so, the stability of his equilibrium is lost, and down he comes. Men have been known to sleep standing without a support, especially on military service, which is the most fatiguing thing in the world; but it is extremely rare, and you may say of a man so standing, even with his feet well spread, that he is already doing a fine athletic feat.

But wait a moment: he desires to go, to proceed, to reach a distant point, and instead of going on all fours, where equilibrium would indeed be stable, what does he do? He deliberately lifts one of his supports off the ground, and sends his equilibrium to the devil; at the same time he leans a little forward so as to make himself fall towards the object he desires to attain. . . .

What you really do, man, when you want to get to that distant place (and let this be a parable of all adventure and of all desire) is to take an enormous risk, the risk of coming down bang and breaking something: you lift one foot off the ground, and, as though that were not enough, you deliberately throw your centre of gravity forward so that you begin to fall.

That is the first act of the comedy.

The second act is that you check your fall by bringing the foot which you had swung into the air down upon the ground again.

That you would say was enough of a bout. Slide the other foot up, take a rest, get your breath again and glory in your feat. But not a bit of it! The moment you have got that loose foot of yours firm on the earth, you use the impetus of your first tumble to begin another one. You get your centre of gravity by the momentum of your going well forward of the foot that has found the ground, you lift the other foot without care, you let it swing in the fashion of a pendulum, and you check your second fall in the same manner as you checked your first; and even after that second clever little success you do not bring your feet both firmly to the ground to recover yourself before the next venture: you go on with the business, get your centre of gravity forward of the foot that is now on the ground, swinging the other beyond it like a pendulum, stopping your third catastrophe, and so on; and you have come to do all this so that you think it the most natural thing in the world! . . .

He is right! I had always thought walking was such a relaxing pastime, but now I know it to be a series of narrowly averted disasters!

After skirting the beech hanger along the foot of the escarpment, at Owlscroft Barn the path rises up into the woods for a while before emerging again and dropping gently down across the fields into Washington. Not the least surprising discovery on this walk is that, although *the book* is, and has been all along, generally accepted as a somewhat bizarre record of a fictional expedition full of extraordinary nonsense and highly amusing accounts of imaginary happenings, there is one consistent thread of authenticity that weaves through its entire length. This is the route that the Four Men followed. Time and again we touch down to the reality of a locality and find that it still exists, sometimes little changed, which convinces us beyond doubt that Belloc trod this ground and knew every inch. Washington and its inn is a case in point:

So all along the road under Chanctonbury, that high hill, we went as the morning broadened: along a way that is much older than anything in the world: a way that leads from old Pevensey Port through the Vale of Glynde and across Cuckmere and across Ouse, and then up to the height of Lewes, and then round the edge of the Combe, and then down on to the ledge below the Downs, making Court House and Plumpton Corner, Clinton, and Hollow Pie Combe (though between these two it branches and meets again, making an island of Wolstonbury Hill), and then on by Poynings and Fulking and Edburton, and so to the crossing of the water and the Fort of Bramber, and so along and along all under the Downs until it passes Arun at Houghton Bridge, and so by Bury and Westburton, and Sutton and Duncton, Graffham and Cocking, and Didling and Harting – all Sussex names and all places where the pure water having dripped through the chalk of the high hills, gushes out in fountains to feed that line of steadings and of human homes. By that way we went, by walls and trees that seemed as old as the old road itself, talking of all those things men talk of, because men were made for speech and for companionship, until we came to the cross roads at Washington.

Now there is a catalogue of magic for any Sussex lover! If for any dreadful reason I found myself unavoidably exiled from my native county, I would have it engraved in poker-work on a piece of Wealden oak and hang it on the wall above the headboard of my bed, and every night murmur it like a prayer until sleep

Washington village, c. 1918, showing the Downs and Chanctonbury Ring in the background

closed around me with visions of that ancient, narrow road and the long, undulating line of the hills under which it winds.

Let future walkers along the time-honoured roadway I trod that morning look out across the flat acres of the Weald with the same satisfaction felt by travellers of old. Let them reflect on all the people that have gone that way before. Travelling in groups to promote a spirit of camaraderie, and to discourage or repel footpads or other undesirable characters along the way, they would have been as mixed and varied company in origins and professions as the Canterbury Pilgrims themselves. They would have kept to this carefully chosen path sufficiently below the crest of the Downs to be sheltered from the wind and weather, and high enough up the lower slopes above the marshy lands to avoid being bogged down in winter. Trudging the path of this ancient road it is easy to be transported in spirit back into days gone by.

I came into Washington not by the same road as Belloc but by a footpath that led me down across a meadow past a little cluster of buildings on my right – the house, stables and cowsheds where old Hedley Baker used to farm. Hedley was a warm-hearted, companionable man. I still treasure a three-legged milking stool with a heart-shaped seat that he took down from a nail in the wall of the cowstall one afternoon and handed to my late wife, Joan, pointing out that three legs were more stable than four on the uneven surface of a meadow or a cowstall floor where the milking was carried out.

He was not from Sussex but prided himself on being 'an Island man from Wight', and, as such, he was given to singing songs from Hampshire, some of them edging toward the risqué. He sang with a rare enthusiasm, his head thrown back, red cheeks aglow and a knowing twinkle in his eye: 'Be I Berkshire? Be I beggary/ Be I come from Fareham.' And all the time he was singing he rolled his fists over and over in front of his chest as if he were hauling in a fishing line.

I reached the road, and there on the opposite side was the Frankland Arms where so many of those songs were sung. But that was nearly fifty years ago.

Almost ninety years ago, on 1 November 1902, the visitors to the inn had been more distinguished. Myself said:

'Have you heard of Washington Inn?'
Grizzlebeard 'Why, yes, all the world has heard of it; and when Washington the Virginian, a general overseas, was worriting his army together a long time ago, men hearing the name would say: "Washington? . . . Washington? . . . I know that name." Then they would remember the inn at Washington, and smile. For fame is of this character. It goes by the sound of names.'
The Poet 'For what, then, is the inn of Washington famous?'
The Sailor 'Not for a song, but for the breeder of songs. You soon shall learn.'

And when we had said that we all went in together, and, in the inn of Washington, he put it to the test what so many men had sung of that ale were true or no. But hardly had the Sailor put his tankard down, when he cried out in a loud voice: 'It is true, and I believe!'

Then he went on further: 'Without any doubt whatsoever this nectar was brewed in the waxing of the moon and of that barley which Brutus brought hither in the first founding of this land! And the water wherein that barley-corn was brewed was May-day dew, the dew upon the grass before sunrise of a May-day morning.'

The Washington Inn that 'all the world has heard of'

I mounted the steps into the bar and, as I had noticed in so many old public houses, although the outside had remained substantially unaltered, the interior had been adapted to meet modern day requirements. Gone are the compartments that used to segregate the squire and his cronies in the big houses from the farm workers and the cottagers, and now we all put our snouts in the same trough, as you might say. Eating also plays a much more important role, so a considerable part of the premises, often the major part, has to be offered as a restaurant or dining area. In spite of this the Frankland Arms is still the Washington Inn, and I sat over a pint cogitating on personal memories of nights of laughter and song under that same roof.

The beer, too, was in excellent condition and my thirst was equal to it, so I had no difficulty whatever in agreeing with the Sailor as he continued in praise of 'Michell's Ale which they sell at Washington':

For it has all the seven qualities of ale, which are:

Aleph	=	Clarity,
Beth	=	Savour,
Gimel	=	A lively hue,
Daleth	=	Lightness,
He	=	Profundity,
Vau	=	Strength retained,

and lastly, Zayin, which is Perfection and The End.

I raised my glass, looked at it, inhaled the bouquet, sipped it, smacked my lips and savoured it, then tipped it up and drained it. Yes, it was all there, and if beauty can be said to be in the eye (and the palate and the throat) of the beholder (and the imbiber), then this nectarean ale was indeed fit for the Gods of Olympus. I recalled another of Belloc's songs which does not appear in *the book*:

> They sell good beer at Haslemere
> And under Guildford Hill.
> At Little Cowfold as I've been told
> A beggar may drink his fill:
> There is a good brew in Amberley too,
> And by the bridge also;
> But the swipes they take in at Washington Inn
> Is the very best beer I know.

(For full version see p. 130.)

That, of course, was in celebration of the ale from Michell's Brewery of Steyning, which ceased to function in 1914. But another fine old Sussex brewery, this time in the eastern half of the county, was Gooche's of Hailsham, whose praises were sung by John Hollamby in 1827:

> O, Gooche's beer your heart will cheer
> And put you in condition;
> The man that will but drink his fill
> Has need of no physician.

Cowfold, c. 1910, where 'a beggar may drink his fill'

'Twill fill your veins, and warm your brains,
And drive out melancholy;
Your nerves 'twill brace, and paint your face,
And make you fat and jolly.

The Foreigners they praise their wine,
('Tis only to deceive us):
Would they come here and taste this Beer
I'm sure they'd never leave us.

The meagre French their thirst would quench,
And find much good 'twould do them;
Keep them a year on Gooche's beer
Their country would not know them.

All you that have not tasted it
I'll have you set about it;
No man with pence and common-sense
Should ever be without it.

In lauding the properties of Sussex beer, Belloc was following a long-established tradition and capturing the character of the old-time Sussex men who have long been renowned for their prodigious consumption of beer. My grandfather, who was brought up in the days when ale was the staple drink of the working man and tea had yet to emerge from the drawing-rooms of the elite, always kept a small barrel in the beer cupboard under the stairs of the cottage. 'Go an' fetch me a jug o' beer out of ol' Bogey, boy, will ye', he would say when he was relaxing in his favourite chair by the fire in the evening. I was adept at 'turning the tap and easing the vent' at a very early age. He had a song that perfectly expressed his devotion to John Barleycorn:

It is of good ale to you I'll sing,
And to good ale I'll always cling,
I like my pot filled to the brim
And I'll drink all you like to bring.
Chorus
O, good ale, thou art my darling,
Thou art my joy both night and morning.

I love you in the early morn,
I love you in daylight, dark or dawn,
And if I'm weary, worn or spent,
I'll turn the tap and ease the vent.
Chorus

It is you that helps me with my work
And from a task I'll never shirk,

If I can get a good home-brew,
And better than one pot I likes two.
Chorus

It is you that makes my friends my foes,
It's you that makes me wear old clothes,
But since you've come so near my nose
That's up you comes and down you goes.
Chorus

And if all my friends from Adam's race
Were to meet me here all in this place,
I could part from all without one tear
Before I'd part from my good beer.
Chorus

And if my wife did me despise
How soon I'd give her two black eyes,
But if she loved me like I love thee,
What a happy couple we should be.
Chorus

You have given me debts and I've often swore
I never would drink strong ale no more,
But you for all that I forgive
And I'll drink strong ale just as long as I live.
Chorus

(Joseph Grimaldi, the Clown (1779–1837) used to sing this song.)

I emerged from the Frankland Arms into bright sunshine, but the wind had built up into gale force. I took the old Worthing road south for a short while before turning west up the street toward the church, which stands in the trees at the top of the hill with its square, castellated tower and a Sussex cap roof inside the parapet. The main roof was of Horsham slabs, which are very much in evidence throughout this part of the county. I walked on westward, crossing over the Worthing to Horsham bypass and following a well-used track, which would be the natural continuation of the old road under the hills.

Out in the open country once again, with the steep beech-covered northern escarpment of the Downs away to my left, I came to Home Farm Cottages where I was greeted by a friendly golden Labrador that seemed pleased to see me. I saw no one, yet had the feeling that someone was watching me.

There are times on a walk like this when there is a long, rather featureless footpath or road to follow for a mile or more that may appear to be somewhat daunting, but I have never found this situation to be tedious. There is always plenty to claim the attention and hold the interest of anyone with the eyes to see and the ability to feel the prevailing mood of the immediate world. These are the little things that are seldom written about, but it would be a pity not to mention the frantic agitation of the foliage in the occasional gusty squalls of wind that eddied here in the lee of the Downs while the full force of the gale was passing overhead, and the impromptu watery showers they caused; the clusters of white cloud sailing like galleons before the wind across the vast blue ocean of sky, and their shadows racing madly over the sunlit Weald beneath, trying to keep pace; the colony of snails tempted by the moisture of a recent shower emerging from their daytime hideouts and pondorously going about their business among the dock leaves at the trackside; and the weazel that scampered across the path ahead of me with an almost serpentine action. These are the sort of pictures that remain in the mind long after a walk is over.

I came to Barns Farm, with its large farmhouse and tall brick chimneys, where, in the garden, the winter vegetables – parsnips, leeks and sprouts – were beginning to thrive and the long row of sweet peas was past its prime and beginning to fade.

Soon the Sussex-capped tower of Sullington Church came into view. Shortly after I was mounting the brick steps into the churchyard, with its ancient yew trees. The church, the manor house, which later became the farmhouse, and the farm huddle closely together in a broad expanse of open country as if to emphasize their close relationship and mutual interdependence. Their association is of many years standing. The church is early English and the long list of more than forty rectors over the years goes back to 1244. According to M.A. Lower, in the reign of Henry VIII the incumbent was Thomas Sackville, 'a student at the gramer scole of thage of 13 – a very young incumbent'. Today he would find himself in *The Guinness Book of Records*.

In an alcove in the tower is an effigy of a knight in armour, reckoned to have been one of the de Covert family, possibly Sir William who was lord of the manor in the late thirteenth century. He lies there in his niche, sadly mutilated by the passage of time with parts of various limbs missing and even his countenance hideously disfigured – far worse than any injuries sustained in battle. Yet still he commands that honour and respect that inspired the high degree of excellence with which his effigy was executed, and still apparent in the finely chiselled detail of his chain mail.

The manor house, too, dates back to the thirteenth century, with walls 5 feet thick in places, many massive beams and attics in one of which was stored the 'Sullington Cheddar' cheeses. I counted five peacocks perching on the walls and adorning the garden.

Down in the farmyard nearby is a splendid old tithe barn, 115 feet long and constructed of huge beams clad with tarred weatherboard on a stone foundation. The interior with its lofty timber work is cathedralesque in appearance and can house more than three hundred tons of sacked corn. The date 1685, carved into one of the beams, is thought to indicate when the barn was restored.

There is an air of antiquity and timelessness that haunts this tiny settlement, set in its wide expanse of farmlands, and I came out on to the lane again with a lingering sense of the distant past. But just three minutes later I was plunged back into the climatic hazards of the immediate present. The heavens opened and a squall of wind and drenching rain descended with alarming ferocity. I fled for the nearest cover – a thick hawthorn hedge under which I found welcome shelter. With the storm raging only yards away I sat in dry and comparative luxury.

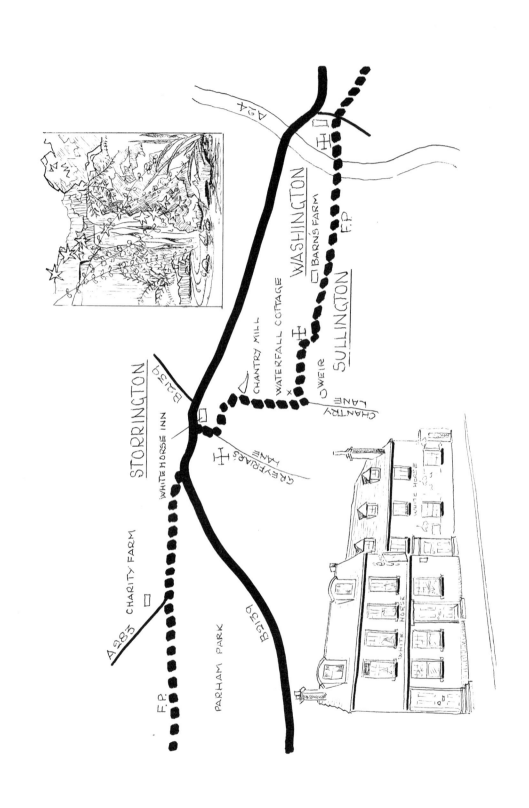

A24

WASHINGTON

BARNS FARM

SULLINGTON

F.P.

CHANTRY MILL

WATERFALL COTTAGE

WEIR

CHANTRY LANE

STORRINGTON

B2139

WHITE HORSE INN

GREYFRIARS LANE

A283 CHARITY FARM

F.P.

PARHAM PARK

B2139

WHITE HORSE

The rain stopped and I emerged into a dripping world. The sun came out and glistened on trees, gate-bars and rooftops like winking diamonds, and I continued on my way, stepping round the deeper puddles. A little under half a mile on I came to Chantry Lane, a tarmacadam road into which I turned right for the last stage of my day's journey up into Storrington. I came out hard by Waterfall Cottage, an attractive property and appropriately named as it was set beside a small cascade of crystal-clear water that tumbled down over a grotto of moss-grown rock and trembling ferns, to make its way down alongside the lane. Just past Chantry Mill, a large building on my right with an extensive millpond not visible from the lower level of the lane, I turned left onto a footpath that brought me out close by the church with its walled churchyard. Picking up Greyfriar's Lane I entered Storrington at about teatime. At the end of the lane was an elaborately carved door opening onto a flight of steps that led up into the grounds of the convent. I was told by a kindly passerby, who noticed my inquisitive interest, that a previous owner who was much travelled had brought it back from his wanderings in the east. That is why it now sits, rather incongruously, in this little Sussex country town.

Just around the corner I booked into the White Horse Hotel where warmth, comfort, a deep, hot bath with large soft towels, an excellent meal with fine wine, and a comfortable bed – in fact, all that a travelling man could possibly wish for – was courteously provided. Here at the White Horse the Four Men met the excitable, lean young huntsman who talked so garrulously about the red horse with the red eyes that had led him such a dance that day. But finding myself in Storrington I was more inclined to meditate on Belloc's poem 'Courtesy':

The Square, Storrington, c. 1907, with the White Horse Hotel on the right

Of Courtesy, it is much less
Than Courage of Heart or Holiness,
Yet in my Walks it seems to me
That the Grace of God is in Courtesy.

On monks I did in Storrington fall,
They took me straight into their Hall;
I saw three pictures on a wall,
And Courtesy was in them all.

The first the Annunciation;
The second the Visitation;
The third the Consolation,
Of God that was Our Lady's Son.

The first was of Saint Gabriel;
On Wings a–flame from Heaven he fell;
And as he went upon one knee
He shone with Heavenly Courtesy.

Our Lady out of Nazareth rode –
It was Her month of heavy load;
Yet was Her face both great and kind,
For Courtesy was in Her Mind.

The third it was our Little Lord,
Whom all the Kings in arms adored;
He was so small you could not see
His large intent of Courtesy.

Our Lord, that was Our Lady's Son,
Go bless you, People, one by one;
My Rhyme is written, my work is done.

And with that reflective and comforting thought I turned my back on the
world for a while and slept like a dormouse.

Storrington to Duncton (12 miles)

Even in 1911 Belloc evidently felt a certain distaste for the developments of the age that, to him, held such dire threats for the world he knew. The leisurely pace and elegance of the late-Victorian and Edwardian English life were in danger, and with an increasing population and consequent proliferation of urban development in rural areas, plus the arrival of the motor car, he felt that the fate of the remoter parts of the county was sealed. That his fears were justified there can be no possible doubt, but the changes he predicted are far more evident in the towns than in the open country.

Storrington is one of only three small towns encountered on this walk. The others are Uckfield and Steyning, so for the greater part of the time anyone following this route, particularly as we are avoiding the busier roads, can be comforted by the fact that the more drastic changes are confined to the urban areas. Once out of the towns there remain many square miles of open, uncluttered countryside, practically unchanged since Belloc passed this way. The cornfields prosper, the sheep grow fat on the downland, the cattle thrive in the water meadows, and the orchards and vineyards ripen in the autumn sunshine. God's in his heaven – all's right with the rural world!

The only obvious difference is that, although the farmlands look much the same as they always did – the hedgerows trimmed, the ditches cleared – you seldom see anyone at work. Gone are the teams of heavy horses pulling ploughs and haywains; the large gangs of mowers and harvesters have been ousted by mechanization, and modern technology has made it possible for one man and a boy to do the work of ten. So the rural scene is practically deserted, but in the towns it is a different story.

Next morning I turned to *the book*. I read how, after the excitable young huntsman had finished his long and detailed account of his hair-raising exploits in the hunting field that day on the devilishly fiery steed he had hired from Mr Benjamin of Petworth, Belloc and his three companions had accompanied him out into the stable yard at the back of the hotel. Here they looked at the sheepish-looking mare for which he had exchanged his original mount to carry him safely home.

I looked out of my bedroom window and tried to visualize the scene as it would have been then: the 'very short ostler of a hard appearance, with the straw of ages in his teeth', going about his stable work; the horses tethered to wall-rings and stamping on the cobbles; the drinking trough; the trusses of hay for fodder and straw for litter; the barrow-loads of dung; the pan-shovels; the long-handled pitchforks; the horse buckets; the curry combs and dandy brushes hanging on the stable wall, and the bottles of horse linament and rolled-up tail bandages on the cobwebbed window ledges. It was difficult. I looked down onto the rooftops of many motor cars of various shapes, sizes and colours that crammed the yard to capacity, standing in rows and tightly packed side by side like sardines in a tin. Every trace of romance had been driven out.

I suppose it is age, but I think a lot of the romance has vanished from life as technology has slowly and insidiously encroached upon us. The light by which I used to read was rated in 'candle-power' not wattage; the car I drove used to have 'horse-power' not 'c.c.'s; the paper on which I wrote was not A4 but good old-fashioned 'foolscap'; and the brewers' drays that once carried 'hogsheads' now deliver ale in 100 litre containers. And what would you rather have as city designations – Shepherd's Bush and Haymarket or 42nd Street and Fifth Avenue? In spite of all the advantages, the clinical efficiency of contemporary life has taken a lot of the warmth and humanity out of living. But I digress.

Well fortified by a huge English breakfast and several cups of good, strong coffee, I left the hotel at about twenty to nine and walked out into the Square where the people of Storrington were already going about their lawful morning business. Shopkeepers were polishing their windows, shop frontages were being swept or hosed down, and goods for sale were on display on forecourts. Cars, buses, delivery vans and bicycles had started their daily, unending dance through the Square, threading and weaving for a clear passage through, while others jostled for parking space, searching for vacant lots at the kerbside like players in a game of musical chairs when the music stops.

I took the road westward toward Pulborough. Belloc tells us he turned off onto the Amberley road and 'passed the heath that is there, leaving the pond upon our right'. This is the route I followed in 1950, the B2139. It was a solitary and

A Southdown flock grazing near Storrington

peaceful walk then and I found time to sit on the bank at the roadside and write in my notebook:

If a man would see Sussex let him see it as I can this February morning, with the watery clouds skimming in from the south-west over Amberley Mount. Let him walk down this road with a stick in his hand, a song on his lips and a heart as big as the sky; the flood-waters acre upon acre stretching up to Pulborough, and before him the range of hill-country from Bury Hill to the wooded slopes of Duncton Down. This is a sight that allows a man to breathe and fills his heart with gladness.

But thirty-four years later, a short time before the walk that is the subject of this book, I had gone down this road again at the same time of day and found it to be a nightmare for the pedestrian. Walking on the offside of the road so as to face the oncoming traffic, as there is no footpath of any description on either side, I had to meet head-on the endless onslaught of a succession of vehicles being driven at terrifying speeds, their drivers presumably striving to reach their various places of employment by nine o'clock. Time after time I was compelled to clamber up on the grassy bank to preserve life and limb, and far from being the lingering, reflective walk I had anticipated it was a continuous battle for survival – an experience I had no wish to repeat.

Instead I kept to the Pulborough road, past the Crown Inn at Cootham, over the little bridge there and then, opposite Charity Farm, I left the main road and went through the white gateway on to the road that leads through the park to Parham House. After a while the road sheers away to the south towards the house, but I followed the footpath straight on, which is fingerposted to Rackham.

Parham House looked grand in the morning sunlight with a flag fluttering proudly at its mast-head. It stands in a beautiful setting of parkland with the swelling green line of the Downs as a backdrop and Rackham Clump for a crown. In the mid-foreground was a circular dove-cote with a conical, tiled roof, topped by a little parapet, which is probably a ventilator, and on top of that a weather-vane. The promontories of the hills glowed in the early eastern light, thrown into a sharp relief against the deep shadows in the rising hollows behind them.

The park was teeming with deer, herding together under the trees or standing around in family groups of half a dozen or so. They were obviously used to the company of people and, although with heads erect on upright necks and ears twitching inquisitively, they regarded me with a rather disdainful interest – as if I were a somewhat inferior specimen of the human race unworthy of their attention; they were not at all put out by my intrusion and calmly resumed their grazing unless I went closer than about 20 yards. Then they would twitch their tails and make a token retreat, springing into a gentle trot of a dozen paces and then carry on, unconcerned.

A short detour would have taken me down to the manor house itself, an elegant Tudor building of grey stone with symmetrically placed gables and a host of splendid brick chimneys, which is open to the public at specific times. The house is the repository for many priceless historic portraits of the great and good over the centuries and is richly furnished with pieces of the most excellent craftsmanship. History and fine art dwell side by side here. Queen Elizabeth I is reputed to have dined at Parham in 1593 on her way to Cowdray, and the delicate sixteenth-century needlework on the four-poster bed in the Great Chamber is, according to tradition, the work of Mary Queen of Scots during the time of her captivity. Cromwellian and Jacobean chairs, huge refectory tables and many smaller items from various periods furnish rooms with tapestry-hung walls, intricate overmantles and heavily moulded ceilings, yet an atmosphere of warmth and intimacy prevails and there is no hint of that impersonal detachment so frequently found in museums and art galleries.

It was until recently the home of Mrs Veronica Tritton, the daughter of the Hon. Clive Pearson, who purchased the house in 1922. Prior to that time it had been in the occupation of the Bisshop family since 1602. It is not in the least surprising that anyone finding themselves firmly ensconced in a truly beautiful home like this in such a glorious setting should be loath to leave it.

North of the house are the laundry and office wings where the archway under the clock-tower leads to an extensive walled garden, well stocked with herbaceous flowers and ornamental shrubs, all immaculately tended. There is also an orchard with ancient gnarled apple and pear trees, and to the west of the garden is an expansive lake.

Back in the main building the tall mullion windows in the Great Hall look southward across the lawns to the little church dedicated to St Peter, where services are still held regularly and the congregation is accommodated in high box-pews. The squire's family box-pew, larger than the rest, is provided with an open fireplace. It is said that a certain squire in times gone by would indicate to the parson in the pulpit that he thought the sermon was over-running time by noisily and ostentatiously stoking the fire, which would be his signal to wind-up and bring the service to a close.

The small village of Parham has long since disappeared. It was demolished at the back end of the eighteenth century, being regarded as 'a source of infection', and the villagers were rehoused at Rackham rather less than a mile to the west where we shall see the Rectory. South of the church the land falls steeply down to Woodmill Pond, which is most probably the pond from which the mutilated body of the unfortunate Richard Hawkins was dragged in 1748. The story of how he met such a tragic end is a reminder that, while the standards of eighteenth-century life in the houses of the wealthy and famous had reached great heights of finesse and gentility, life at a lower level could be crude, violent and downright brutish.

One January day in 1748 Hawkins, a farm labourer of Yapton, was threshing corn in a barn near his home when he was approached by two men who were strangers to him. One was Jeremiah Curtis, a butcher from Hawkhurst, and the other John Mills, alias Smoker, of Trotton. Both were deeply involved in smuggling activities along the south coast. They were ruthless and vicious men. Mills was a member of a gang that had recently broken into the Customs House at Poole and retaken a consignment of tea that they had smuggled in from Guernsey and which had been seized by the Excise men. During this operation he had been involved in the murder of an informant.

They had cached some bags of the run tea near the barn at Yapton and had ridden over that day to pick it up, but, finding that some of it was missing and seeing Hawkins at work in the barn close by, they accused him of taking it. He denied all knowledge of the tea but they refused to accept his story. Holding a pistol to his head they threatened him and conveyed him, riding pillion to Mills, to an alehouse known as the Dog and Partridge on Slindon Common, about five miles away.

There he was taken into a private parlour and viciously assaulted. He was repeatedly beaten, kicked and whipped 'over the face, head, arms, belly and private parts', until at last he admitted that the tea was in the possession of his father- and brother-in-law, the Cockrels who kept a public house at Yapton. They left him and went to find the Cockrels, but while they were away Hawkins died of the horrendous injuries they had inflicted upon him.

Hearing of his death they returned to Slindon without the Cockrels. Slinging the bruised and battered body of their victim over a horse's back, they carried it to Parham Park, a distance of some twelve miles, tied large rocks to it and threw it in Sir Cecil Bisshop's pond, where it was discovered about nine months later.

Curtis fled the country but Mills was subsequently apprehended, found guilty and finally hanged in chains on a gibbet on Slindon Common, close to the scene of the dastardly crime. The whole of this hideous drama unfolded while life inside Parham House pursued the gracious tenor of its ways only a few hundred yards away from where the body was found.

As I walked I looked in vain for the heronry for which Parham was once noted. Landowners were fiercely proud of the fact that a colony of herons had exercised their whimsical prerogative and decided to nest and breed in the trees on their estates. The owners of Parham were among the chosen few. The Parham herons had an interesting history. They originally hailed from Wales, but in the early seventeenth century were brought up to Penshurst in Kent where their progeny remained for over two hundred years. They eventually migrated to Michelgrove, a journey of 70 miles, remaining there for twenty years. Then, as a result of some of the trees supporting their nests being felled, they flew over the hill to make their home at Parham, four miles away. This happened in 1831 and they were still happily nesting there until about 1944. I know this to be so because I remember the wave of shock and horror that shook the locals when a Canadian soldier was reputed to have shot one to supplement his supper ration. Parham House was at the time occupied by the Canadian Army. The ancient stairways and panelled walls were boarded over to prevent excess wear and tear and the valuable paintings put in store.

I left Parham through another white gateway between the two West Lodges and turned south on the road to Rackham. I was now on the fringes of that area of country that was for Belloc, as it is for so many of us, the very heart of all that is best in Sussex. These are the scenes of which he dreamt as he sat before the fire and drank 'that port of theirs' at the George Inn at Robertsbridge.

I came to a gap in the hedge and I leant on the gate there, looking out westward onto a panoramic vista of absolute delight. The day was fair and of that rare quality that only September can offer, and the deep silence of the countryside enveloped the morning like a benediction. How near to heaven is this valley where the meandering river Arun winds its way through cattle-cropped water-meadows toward the sea. Was this the small plot of earth upon which the Almighty breathed on the very first day of Creation? Is that why ever since the waters have run clearer, the grass has grown greener and the breezes blown softer and sweeter than anywhere else on earth? God's mark is all around; it is a blessed country.

On both sides of the river, herds of Friesians grazed and chewed the cud in the flat, green meadows between the grid-line brooks, and beyond, the valley ran smoothly away to the foot of that noble range of downland draped with the famed West Sussex beech-hangers – all along the hills from Bury past Westburton, Bignor and Barlavington to Duncton Down.

About half a mile south, on the road I had forsaken, on the third day out on the original walk, Myself had said:

When we get over that lift of land upon the Amberley road before us we shall see Arun a long way off between his reeds, and the tide tumbling in Arun down towards the sea. We shall see Houghton and Westburton Hill, and Duncton further along, and all the wall of them, Graffham and Barlton, and so to Harting, which is the end where the county ceases and where you come to shapeless things. All this is our own country, and it is to see it at last that we have travelled so steadfastly during these long days.

Soon after the rain began to fall, but:

we had come to such a height of land that the rain and the veils of it did but add to the beauty of all we saw, and the sky and the earth together were not like November, but like April, and filled us with wonder. At this place the flat water-meadows, the same that are flooded and turned to a lake in mid-winter, stretch out a sort of scene or stage, whereupon can be planted the grandeur of the Downs, and one looks athwart that flat from a high place upon the shoulder of Rackham Mount to the broken land, the sand hills, and the pines, the ridge of Egdean side, the uplifted heaths and commons which flank the last of the hills all the way until one comes to the Hampshire border, beyond which there is nothing. This is the foreground of the gap of Arundel, a district of the Downs so made that when one sees it one knows at once that here is a jewel for which the whole county of Sussex was made, and the ornament worthy of so rare a setting. And beyond Arun, straight over the flat where the line against the sky is highest, the hills I saw were the hills of home.

I walked down past Rackham House and the Rectory, turning right to Amberley, and at Crossgates I found the Sportsman Inn open and ready to do business. There was but one other occupant of the bar, Peter Hamilton, a man of four-score or thereabouts. He was a local, judging by his dress and accent. I invited him to join me in a drink and we sat there for a while in a beer-sipping silence as I mentally recalled the last occasion when I was under that roof.

It was in 1953 early one Saturday evening in August. I was travelling the area for the BBC, making field recordings of traditional singers in their natural habitat or good specimens of local dialect for the Permanent Library. It was an extremely hot day and I popped in to slake a troublesome thirst I had contracted during the afternoon's activities. I was taken aback at the sight that met my eyes.

The small room was dressed from floor to ceiling with a variety of flowers, fruits and vegetables arranged decoratively on every available surface. The mantleshelf, tables and window ledges were covered with prize specimens of parsnips, carrots, runner beans, cauliflowers, apples, pears, plums and peaches, while bunches of asters, sweet williams and antirrhinums in vases made the air sweet with their perfume. It looked like a cross between a village flower and vegetable show and a Harvest Festival service in the church, and that is precisely what it turned out to be.

At one end of the room on a table, with a pristine white linen cloth draped down to the floor, stood a crucifix flanked by two candles in tall brass candlesticks. To the left of this makeshift altar stood a fat sheaf of barley, and to the right a sheaf of wheat, rich, golden and beneficent. There were sixteen or so villagers present, and a tall man in vestments, the local incumbent, was presiding. A short service was about to begin and I was given permission to record it.

The simple sincerity with which the service was conducted, the reverent attention given to every word of the address and the prayers, and the enthusiasm with which the old favourite harvest hymns were sung were truly impressive; more so, perhaps, because of the unhallowed premises in which we were worshipping. Licensed premises are more readily associated with the forces of darkness, therefore the impact was the greater. The stars always shine brighter on a dark night with no moon.

The company was made up of men and women whose lives were closely bound up with nature and the stubborn soil of the earth from which they wrested a living. Shepherds, waggoners, farm labourers and their womenfolk have more reason than their town-bred cousins to praise the Lord at harvest time. It is the end to which their year-long labours have been directed, and no one appreciates more than those that turn the furrow, sow the seed and reap the corn how much the success of a season depends on forces beyond the control of man. It did one's heart good to hear them singing. Part of the service was later broadcast on a BBC radio programme, *The Countryside In . . .*

I broke the silence. 'I was last in here,' I mused, 'about thirty-five years ago.'

'Yeah, I know,' replied my companion slowly, 'you recorded an 'arvest thanksgiving service for the BBC.'

I turned to him in astonishment. 'However did you know that?' I queried.

'I was 'ere,' he replied, as if that explained everything.

I came to Amberley at about noon. What can be said of this charming little village that has not already been written? I wandered round the narrow street between the stone-walled and white-washed cottages nestling under venerable roofs, where wallflowers lived up to their name and sprouted from cracks in the masonry. Gardens were ablaze with late-blooming flowers, vegetable plots were rich with harvest, and a group of young Sussex bullocks were fattening on deep litter in a walled cattle yard. Occasionally the smell of cooking drifted out through an open window and there prevailed that indefinable atmosphere of hospitality and homeliness that seems to be engendered by long-established human habitation. In ancient villages like this – where over the centuries fires have burned brightly on the hearth-stones, thatches have kept homes warm and dry and the well-springs have run constant and clear, while generations of men and women have brought up their families and lived out their lives – you will find a reassuring sense of permanence not evident in more recently developed settlements. I first came under the spell of Amberley in 1940:

At Amberley the days are free,
The skylark tops the Mount so bare,
But cannot fly near half so high
As soars my heart when I am there.

What joys we find; what peace of mind;
What sights for country-loving eyes
Unfold again along the lane
At every twist and dip and rise.

How sweet the store through cowstall
    door
Of locust beans baked brown and hard,
And how benign the munching kine
Within the aromatic yard.

Grey herons glide across the wide
And lonely Brooks where plovers call;
In churchyard green the tombstones
    lean,
And dream beside the castle wall.

How like a balm the air of calm
Inside the ancient cottage door;
The wheel-back chairs, the crooked
    stairs,
And shelves weighed down with
    books galore.

What sight can match 'neath hanging
    thatch,
The view of lawns through latticed
    panes;
And what intrude upon the mood
The steady-ticking clock maintains.

At Amberley the days are free,
The skylark tops the Mount so
    bare,
But cannot fly near half so high
As soars my heart when I am there.

In the Black Horse by the square I met another Amberley man in his late seventies. He was sitting in the corner of the bar beneath several sepia photographs of old local farming scenes, with the peak of his tweed cap shoved back off his forehead exposing to full view his beaming, apple-cheeked countenance, which wore a gentle and genial look. He regarded me with a friendly but shrewd eye and we exchanged pleasantries. He had on the table before him a partly consumed pint of cider, which, at my invitation, he quickly drained and allowed me to replenish. I took my own drink and sat down alongside him, and we talked of this and that as well-met strangers will.

The matter of age cropped up as it does from time to time between those who are no longer young, and his views on the matter were both original and heartening. 'You never don't warnt t' grumble about gittin' old, 'cos it's better 'an dying young – an' that's the only option.' And, 'Anyway, you're not the only one gittin' long in the tooth – so's ev'ry-one else.' And finally, 'Wal, I reck'n a man o' eighty stands a better chance o' livin' t' be a hundred than a man o' fifty.'

His name, or at least that by which he is known locally, was Cider Bob. He admitted to being renowned for his insatiable thirst for the fermented juice of the apple, particularly as a young man, and told me how he came to be known by such an unusual nickname. At one time the landlord of the pub used to make some really ferocious cider from local apples, and so fearsome was the alcoholic strength of this beverage that on a Saturday night he would make an offer that the first man who could drink three consecutive pints of it should be given a fourth one on the house. The average man would find that two, or perhaps two and half, pints would be as much as he could carry, but Bob had such an astonishing capacity and qualified for a free pint so regularly that he was excluded from the contest and the landlord was obliged to add a rider to his original offer – 'But that don't include Cider Bob.' And so the name stuck with him.

I left the village and about 400 yards to the south I picked up the original route again.

> Our business now was to see Arun in his strength, in that place where he is already full of the salt sea tide, and where he rolls so powerful a water under the Bridge and by Houghton Pit and all round by Stoke Woods and so to Arundel and the sea.
>
> Then we looked at that river a little while, and blessed it, and felt each of us within and deeply the exaltation of return, the rain still falling on us as we went. We came at last past the great chalk pit to the railway, and to the Bridge Inn which lies just on this side of the crossing of Arun.

I passed the entrance to the 'great chalk pit', which is now Amberley Chalk Pits Museum, an extensive open air museum of southern industrial history. Here the past is comprehensively put on display, including earlier forms of road and rail transport and ancient farming implements. Old-fashioned skills are brought to life by demonstrations of charcoal burning, hurdle making, pottery, and all the crafts of the blacksmith, wheelwright, cobbler and baker.

Before crossing the river at Houghton I went into the Bridge Inn for an early lunch and turned once more to *the book*:

> When we had all four come in out of the rain into Mr Duke's parlour at the Bridge Inn, and we had ordered beer and had begun to dry ourselves at the fire, the Sailor said: 'Come, Grizzlebeard, we promised to tell the stories of our first loves when we came to Arun; and as you are much the oldest of us do you begin.

Thus in that small bar parlour did they beguile the hour and forget the rain outside. First Grizzlebeard, then the Sailor, followed by the Poet told the tales of how love had first come into their lives. Finally it was the turn of Myself to unburden his heart. Some of the romantic experiences put into the mouths of the first three might well have been true in that they had played a greater or lesser part in Belloc's own life. However, the veracity of Myself's assertion that his first love was money is called sharply into question by his known ambivalent attitude towards financial affairs in general and, in particular, his grandson's account of having seen him stagger out of the Black Horse in the Carfax at Horsham one night, and, in a cynical, drunken gesture, scatter a roll of pound notes into the gutter and push them along with his blackthorn stick until they disappeared down the drain. That was not the behaviour of an avaricious man.

I fell to thinking how much the interior of the inn had changed since I first knew it in 1940. At that time it was obviously much the same as it had been in 1902. The small parlour with its black cast-iron fireplace and the dark-brown paint on the doors and window frames had been there, little doubt, when Belloc called. So many details of this part of the county are still crystal clear in my mind for they hold a special place in *my* heart, too.

It was here that *I* first found love, which is another way of saying that here I first found life. Here it was, with the girl who was to be my partner for almost

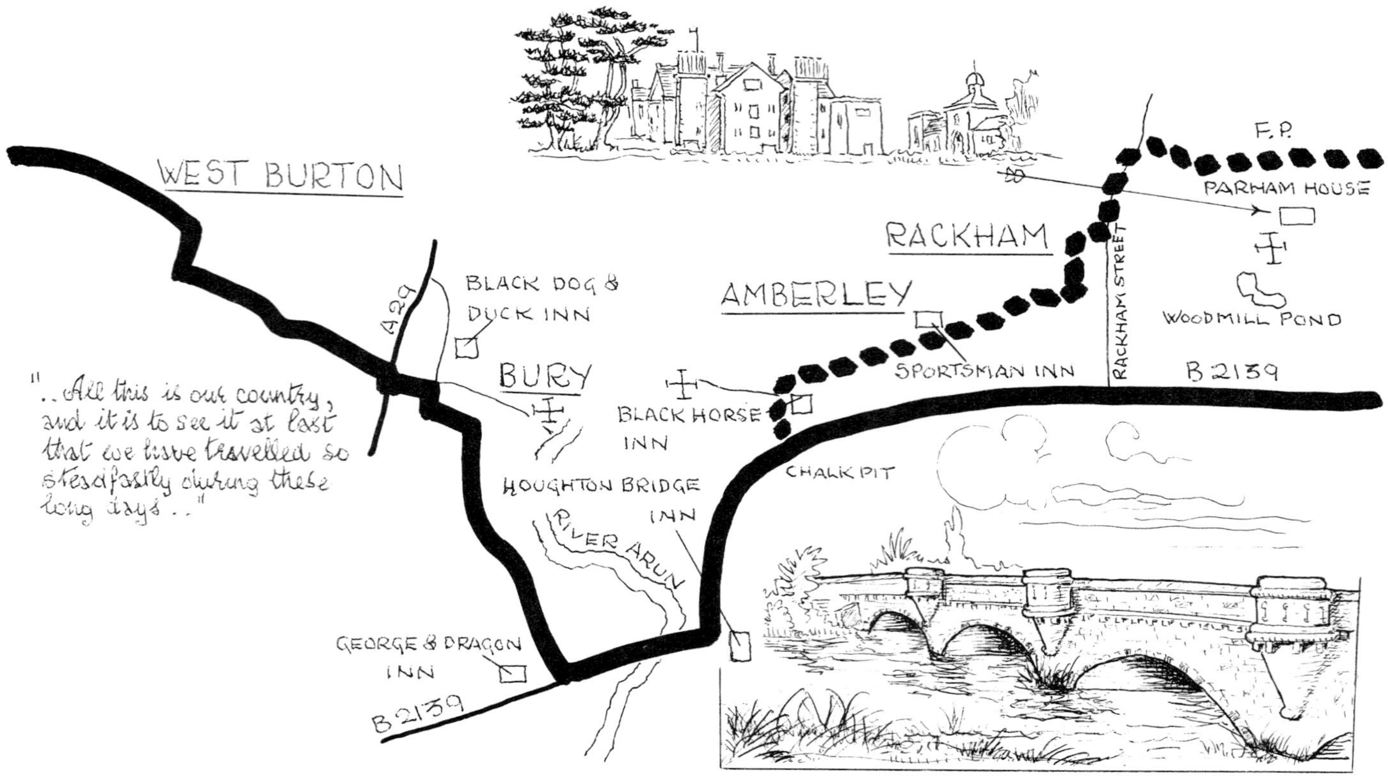

WEST BURTON

"... All this is our country, and it is to see it at last that we have travelled so steadfastly during these long days ..."

BURY

A29

BLACK DOG & DUCK INN

HOUGHTON BRIDGE

RIVER ARUN

GEORGE & DRAGON INN

B2139

AMBERLEY

BLACK HORSE INN

CHALK PIT

SPORTSMAN INN

B2139

RACKHAM

RACKHAM STREET

F.P.

PARHAM HOUSE

WOODMILL POND

Houghton Bridge, which carries the B2139 over the river Arun

fifty years until her death, that I discovered the little churches, the quiet inns and the forgotten paths through the woods and along the river bank that made all the world seem young and set our two hearts dancing to the fiddle tunes of love.

We walked the High Woods where the scent of harvest was seasoned with the brine of the sea; we dreamed on the river bank and wondered what life was all about; and we planned for the future – in so far as it is possible for any of us to make plans in this uncertain world – over mugs of ale in remote country inns that still catered almost exclusively for the local men, where saloon bars had not been invented and our presence as 'furriners' was regarded as a novel and beguiling diversion. The whole of this part of the county is rich with poignant memories that still remain sharply etched on my mind.

I remember the river at Bury where we shouted across to old Bob Dudden, the ferryman, who was sawing logs in the garden of his cottage on the opposite side. But we shouted in vain until at last the log dropped to the ground. Then, straightening his back and lighting his pipe, all the while effecting not to have heard our call, he presently looked up with feigned surprise, walked leisurely to the wooden steps on his side of the water, untied the painter of his punt and slowly paddled across to pick us up.

It was all a charade, but it was played out with such good-humoured grace, and it carried such a salutary lesson for anyone more accustomed to the headlong rush of urban life, that the fare of two old-fashioned brown pennies he diffidently asked for seemed pitifully inadequate. Yet he resolutely refused to take more, thereby driving home another lesson. To meet a man like Bob the Ferryman was an edifying experience. In the course of less than ten minutes, in his quiet, unhurried way, he had firmly knocked on the head two of the commonest of human weaknesses – impatience and avarice.

At about that time, as a young but not overzealous policeman in Worthing, I was once berated by a senior officer for a lack of initiative. 'Haven't you got any ambition, boy?' he taunted. 'Yes, sir,' I replied, 'to be the ferryman at Bury.' Have you ever seen a nonplussed police inspector?

Up in the village of Bury, where the sign of the Black Dog and Duck swings in the branches of a huge walnut tree, we sat in a circle of friendly, sunburnt faces and listened while they told us of illicit swan suppers to mark the end of the cricket season; and of the mead with a kick like a donkey made by a local farmer, the heady effects of which a certain constable, who had called to check the farm registers (and who later achieved equally heady rank), had to sleep off under a haystack. We heard, too, of how the pub got its name. It was originally known as the Black Dog, and the sign bore a picture of Jim, a black retriever, who belonged to Mr Henly, the landlord. They were inseparable companions and were so frequently seen coming up off the Brooks, he with a gun over his arm and Jim with a mallard in his jaws, that someone suggested that a duck should be added to the sign as you seldom saw one without the other, from which time the pub became known as the Black Dog and Duck.

Inside on the parlour wall hung a notice, brown with tobacco smoke:

> Friendly advice. Speak Honourably.
> Call Frequently. Drink Moderately.
> Part Friendly. Go home quietly.
> Let these lines be no man's sorrow,
> Pay today and Trust tomorrow.

On winter evenings we played tippet in the Woodman's Arms at Hammerpot with old 'Smithy', the lugubrious landlord with the drooping moustache, and his cronies until the combined heat from a great log fire and the low-slung oil lamp suspended from a beam overhead beaded our foreheads with sweat. In summer we walked up the river path to the George and Dragon at Burpham. Here, Ada West, the charming and gracious landlady with a tremendous goitre, served ale in quart pots and told us of the days when, as a small girl in the 1860s, she used to help her parents serve up over sixty pints of beer every midday to the navvies who were laying the railway through the Arun valley. And we prayed and gave thanks for all these things in the tiny church by the river at South Stoke, where the interior walls are of chalk and the altar rail holds memories close to the heart.

Here in the parlour of the Bridge Inn Grizzlebeard had said:

> But since the rain is over let us be off again. It is November: the days are brief; and the light will not last us long. Let us press forward over Arun, and pursue our westward way beneath the hills.

> So we did as he bade us, crossing the long bridge and seeing the water swirling through on the strong brown tide, and so along the causeway, and up the first ride into Houghton, where is that little inn, 'St George and the Dragon', at which King Charles the Second, the first King of England to take a salary and be a servant, drank as he fled from Worcester many years ago.

On the sturdy, stone-built bridge I paused to watch the dark waters glide

The George and Dragon Inn at Houghton, where King Charles II stopped to drink as he fled from Worcester

smoothly below me, eddying round the cut-waters and carrying clumps of grass and river-weed along on the current. The meadows at the side were grazed down close, leaving only small patches of yellow ragwort here and there. I walked along the causeway and felt a strange satisfaction in seeing the speeding motor cars brought to a standstill by a herd of cows coming in from the fields. Up the gentle slope that is the beginning of Houghton Hill I soon came to the George and Dragon, a flint-built inn with a low lichened roof of brown tiles. It was in 1651 that the excitement of Charles II's visit had stirred the pulses of the locals, since which time it had settled down once again to pursue the even tenor of its ways.

Retracing my steps for a short distance I turned north into Houghton Lane, and a pleasant mile between the grassy banks and hedgerows brought me into Bury. Along this road the four-in-one Belloc must have strode:

And we went on that ancient way, that hollow way, which the generations and the generations rolling upon wheels and marching on leather, all on their way to death, have worn down so far below the level of the brown, ploughed lands.

Cottage, Houghton Lane

What changes would he find if he were here today? Physically very little. It is in the subtler things of life that his predictions have been most accurate: the kind of people and their mode of living that have changed so drastically, and even these changes have come about slowly over a long period. After all, it is nearly ninety years since he was here.

I was just coming up into Bury village and duly arrived in the Square, the focal point of four roads and the village centre where the general stores and post office supply the village's needs. I had arrived there on the road from the south; to the east is the cul-de-sac that leads past several pleasant houses to the church and to the river bank where the ferry used to ply. The street to the north passes some splendid examples of property conversion and on up the hill to the Black Dog and Duck Inn, running out eventually on to the main road to Pulborough and beyond. I took the road to the west, past the stores and a large grey stone house which looks older than its years, where John Galsworthy once lived.

Crossing the main road, the A29, I turned toward Westburton. This is a very pleasant road to walk along and Westburton is a dreamy place of stone walls and thatched cottages, five-bar gates and open farmlands, not forgetting the spreading cedar tree that reaches out protectively over the road. Arthur Beckett tells us in the 'Spirit of the Downs' that he got a lift through here in a horse and cart in the early years of this century. The driver said of Westburton, 'No sir; nothing ever 'appens there – leastwise I have never 'eard tell of anything.' When pressed as to how the local people spent their time, he replied, 'They do nothing – only works.' It was quiet; there was no one abroad and a monastic calm prevailed. Judging from what I saw that afternoon they don't even work now.

I like to think of Belloc walking this road and pausing from time to time, as inspiration came, to scribble notes with a stub of pencil on any scrap of paper he happened to have in his pocket. This is the way he worked. He was undoubtedly the sort of man who would have spurned the use of the sophisticated aids that are on offer to the writers of today, even if they had been available, and his rather casual approach to his art is most endearing, particularly as it produced such eminently excellent results.

Even *the book* that is the subject of these pages was written, at least in part, by these unconventional means. J.B. Morton in his *Hilaire Belloc: A Memoir*, writes:

Once when we were going through some papers at King's Land I found several pages torn out of a picture paper – I think it was the *Illustrated London News*. There was writing scrawled all over the pictures and over the margins. 'What's all this?' I asked. 'Let's have a look,' he said. I handed the sheets to him, and he deciphered the writing. 'It's part of *The Four Men*,' he said. And we found the original sketch of the amusing map of Sussex from that book. He asked me if I would like it, and it now hangs in my study at home.

I was on the Belloc road:

We went past Bury to Westburton, and still onwards to the place where some dead Roman had his palace built, near the soldiers' road, in a place that looks at a great hollow of the Downs and is haunted by the ruin of fifteen hundred years.

About three quarters of a mile west of Westburton a gateway on the north side of the road allows access to the remains of the Roman villa. These are now protected by low flint-walled buildings, which from the road look like cattle sheds and stand away to the north in the middle of open farmlands. These ruins were

Off to the Downs at Houghton, c. 1907

discovered in 1811 when the ploughshare unearthed a number of shards that turned out to be part of a tessellated pavement in a remarkably good state of preservation and of extremely high artistic merit. Excavations unearthed the remains of courts, baths, a hypocaust, beautifully decorated floors and the foundations of an extensive villa covering about four acres. It is thought to have been the residence of a Roman colonial governor of considerable wealth and influence, for it is on the route of Stane Street, the Roman road from Regnum (Chichester) to Londinium, which descends the wooded steepness of the Downs a quarter of a mile away to the south.

Such riches of ancient history imbue the air with a sense of antiquity. To the east the chain of hills, spur after spur, diminish into the blue distance of Chanctonbury, and the Roman ghosts that one feels must inhabit this place would feel quite at home. But, perhaps, on seeing their proud straight highway to the capital overgrown with trees and eroded by arable farmlands, and the palatial villa demolished and reduced to one or two sections of mosaic flooring and a few under-floor heating pipes, they might be tempted to think there had been more regress than progress since the days of Imperial Rome.

I turned up into Bignor village, passing what is possibly the most depicted house in Sussex, the exquisite fifteenth-century yeoman's cottage with its sturdy timbers set in walls of flint, stone and bricks laid in English, Flemish and

Yeoman's cottage, Bignor

Bury, c. 1907, showing a signpost pointing the way to Westburton, Bignor and Sutton, the route followed by Belloc

herringbone bond, and its over-hanging upper storey windows looking out from under a deep brow of thatch. The two front doors are reached up a short flight of stone steps that at one time had to be negotiated by the village housewives, for this used to be the local grocer's shop.

A little farther on I passed Bignor Church where the tiled lych-gate roof is supported on four stout, eight-inch corner posts of oak. The church is small with a little shingled spire at the west end. Going down the steep incline to Bignor Mill I was practically looking down the chimneys of a rich man's house, for the mill has been converted into an enviably lovely residence surrounded by beech and ash trees, which were still in their summer splendour.

I came to the White Horse Inn at Sutton. It was a pleasing sight there under the trees at the junction where three lanes meet. Standing in the obtuse angle between two of them and looking directly down the third, the golden light of the afternoon sunshine warmed its iron-stone walls to the colour of ripened wheat, and its reflection winked from the small panes in the bedroom windows. White-painted window boxes brimmed over with salvias and godetias, and nasturtiums trailed streamers from those on the upper floor.

The joints between the courses of stone blocks in the walls were studded with small chippings of the same stone that protruded like frost nails in a horseshoe. They were quite decorative but also formed small drip-stones to carry the rain water away from the face of the blocks. This is called 'garreting'.

At the top of a short flight of brick steps was a door that was familiar to me, for here until a short time ago we used to hold a monthly 'Sing Around'. A small gathering of friends were in the habit of meeting here to spend an evening of traditional music and song, which was run on the old-fashioned lines of the 'sing, say or pay' evenings enjoyed in the taprooms of old. The company sat in a ring around the room and each in his or her turn would be called upon to give a song, a recitation or anecdote, in default of which a forfeit was demanded in the shape of a fine. In the event we were all keen enthusiasts of traditional entertainment and there was never a shortage of eager performers, certainly no defaulters, so there would have been a paucity of funds in the kitty had we not agreed to make voluntary contributions into a basin on the counter to cover food and drink for the evening.

I remember the last of the pub sing songs in the early 1930s when a few of the old men of my grandfather's time were still singing the songs that had been handed down from earlier days, and the nights at the White Horse were as near to those of sixty years ago as it is possible to get these days. They were certainly as enjoyable. Here we were still singing the old songs, but this time with the younger generation – my son John and his wife Lynne, and my daughter Jill and her husband Jon – and listening to other tunes and songs of the same vintage performed by other young people.

Will, a small, warm-natured man with nimble fingers, would sit in a low chair by the fireplace playing a concertina on his knee with a lively rhythm that set toes tapping all round the room. He sat like a little gnome with his eyes tight shut behind steel-rimmed glasses and would be entirely lost to his surroundings, carried away on the wings of his music to a *Merrie England* world of nymphs and shepherds, where many a Colin and his Rosalind stepped the light fantastic on the village green. He carried us all with him.

A game of dominoes would be going on in a corner at the far end of the room, the players cocooned in a cloud of blue tobacco smoke and engrossed in their game to the exclusion of everything else that was going on around them. Carefully considered pieces were placed on the table from time to time, pipes were puffed at leisurely intervals and beer in the glasses at their elbows lowered sip by sip. At the end of each game scores were notched up on a large oak cribbage board with brass pegs, but never a word was spoken. It was a solemn business.

The walls of the room were lined with match-boarding, a method of excluding draughts and bringing an old building up to date – very popular around the turn of the century. The men who used inns like this in those days demanded nothing in the way of decoration, and bars and taprooms were purely functional – a place where a man could find warmth and company after a heavy day's work behind the plough, or up on the hills with his flock where the wind and rain swept in off the sea. Floors were of bare boards or, even better suited to withstand the scraping of heavy boots, flagstone or brick. It was not until the 1930s, when fewer and fewer people worked on the land and the big drift of rural populations to the towns began, that country landlords felt obliged, or perhaps were forced, to make their inns quaint and 'olde worlde' to attract the ever-increasing car trade. This little place was a survivor from those years.

On the wall was a smoke-stained price list about forty years out of date listing bitter at a shilling a pint when that which we were drinking was nearer a pound. Also on the wall was a cross-stitch sampler framed in *passe partout*: 'There is not upon earth so good a thing as an inn'. I wondered who had admired the Sailor's assertion so much as to quote him in such a devoted and painstaking manner.

Arthur Beckett had come in here in about 1908 and it would be perfectly reasonable to assume that he saw it precisely the same as it was up to a year or two

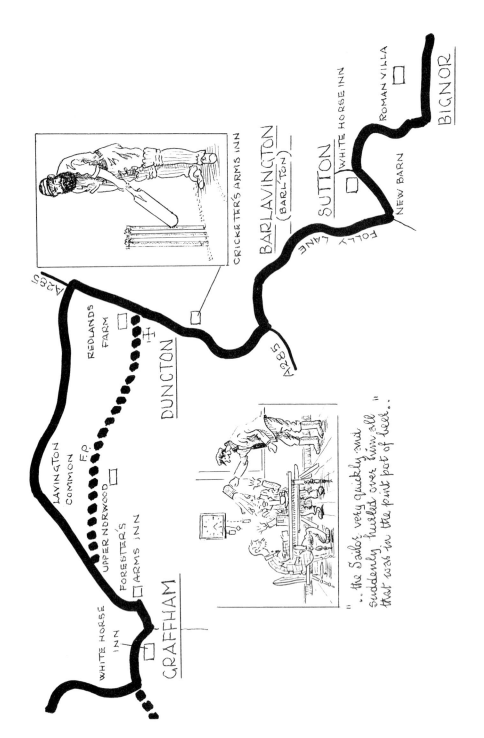

GRAFFHAM

WHITE HORSE INN

FORESTER'S ARMS INN

UPPER NORWOOD

F.P.

LAVINGTON COMMON

A285

DUNCTON

REDLANDS FARM

A285

CRICKETER'S ARMS INN

BARLAVINGTON (BARLTON)

FOLLY LANE

SUTTON

WHITE HORSE INN

NEW BARN

ROMAN VILLA

BIGNOR

".. the Sailor very quickly and suddenly hurled over him all that was in the pint pot of beer.."

ago. One thing that struck him most unfavourably and of which we saw no sign was the 'foul language of these bucolic tosspots', which offended his sense of decorum, particularly in the presence of the innkeeper's youthful daughter. There were, however, similarities between his times and ours, but even then with distinctions. There was, for instance, music and singing. Beckett described the songs as being 'shouted by the raucous-voiced, beer-stimulated crowd of villagers in the inn at Sutton', but we enjoyed singing that was both orderly and melodious.

Bob was a native of West Sussex, had a pleasant relaxed singing voice and an extensive repertoire of Sussex songs, most of which, in the finest tradition, he learnt from his mother. Of above average height, he had a frank and straightforward manner, which was reflected in his talking and singing, with a direct look in his eye and a generous mouth always ready to split into a wide grin. He was a colourful character, and his curly hair and bushy side-whiskers gave him something of a late-Victorian look, and in his blue reefer jacket with brass buttons he needed only a little help from a pair of earrings and a shiny peaked cap to be taken for the first mate on a whaler at the time of Moby Dick. He moved easily into a song without fuss or preamble, and his voice was tuneful and nicely modulated – relaxed and almost conversational. He had plenty of support in the choruses.

Presently Sheila, the landlady, and Tricia, her daughter, would come in with plates piled high with freshly cut sandwiches and hot jacket potatoes halved and topped with butter and toasted cheese, and this would ensure a short period of enforced silence. But the round of music and song would quickly be resumed. Marilyn was petite and pretty with a great mop of dark hair, and her dulcet tones rivalled the blackbird in May.

Vic was a big man, round of face, rotund in figure, and he wore spectacles with circular lenses. He was a musician in the true sense of the word and approached the matter on a more scholarly level than most of us. His researches and learned books and essays have contributed richly to our knowledge of sacred and secular parochial music, but his academic achievements were no hindrance to his enjoyment of music on a humbler level. He was the possessor of a telling tenor voice that was equally adept at adding touches of drama or humour to a song when required, and when Will and he joined forces on concertinas – Will leading on the Anglo and Vic providing an intricate obliggato on the Duet – ill-matched though they may have been physically, their music blended to perfection.

These evenings – and they are still going on, though not at Sutton – reassure me that Sussex traditional music and song is safe in such hands as these.

The Old Songs

O, you can moan in a plaintive tone
Your gormless modern tune,
But I will roar along the shore
Beneath a blood-red moon,
And songs that Nelson's sailors sang
Shall ring across the wave,
And fifty thousand sailor-men shall join the chorus brave,
The chorus brave and tarry that savours of the sea,
For fifty thousand sailor-men shall rise to sing with me.

Chorus
The old songs, yes, the old songs
That gave our fathers joy,
The songs they sang till the welkin rang
When Nelson was a boy.

Or in the dusty sunlit barn
A farmer's song I'll sing,
A country rhyme to the rhythmic time
Of flails that thump and swing,
All up and down the threshing floor
To win the golden grain,
And fifty thousand threshermen shall join the bold refrain,
The bold refrain and fearless that springs from English soil,
And fifty thousand threshermen shall join my song of toil.

Chorus

Or in the depths of cellar cool
Reclining on a bench,
When I've dispersed an honest thirst
That ale alone can quench,
I'll wake the vaulted echoes wide
In praise of barley brew,
And fifty thousand drinking men shall join the chorus true,
The chorus true and hearty of hops and barley-malt,
For fifty thousand drinking men shall prove they're worth their salt.

The old songs, yes the old songs
That gave our fathers joy,
The songs they sang till the welkin rang
When Nelson was a boy
Will echo onward down the years
And never, never fade,
For honest English singing-men will never be afraid
To raise their lusty voices, their spirits to revive,
And sing to all eternity,
'We're glad that we're alive!'

Westward from Sutton I came across The Old Jam Man standing by a rather rickety stand outside his cottage, with an awning of green canvas sheltering an impressive display of bottled pickles, jams and sauces. He is well known in the district and patronized by those who appreciate good quality jams and really hot pickles and condiments, like horseradish with Tobasco and chilli sauces of searing intensity. At New Barn I turned north toward Barlavington, referred to by Belloc as Barl'ton, and up between high banks and hedgerows where in winter little streams of water from field drainage systems trickle down through natural roadside grottos with ferns, moss and ground ivy clinging to the sandstone rocks.

Soon the road runs close under the northern slopes of the Downs, which rise sharply to the left with Duncton Mill Farm close by down to the right. A backward glance reveals the long range of downland running eastward almost along to Steyning some 15 miles away.

It was hereabouts that the Sailor sang his outrageous carol, which Grizzlebeard called 'rank blasphemy', but which the singer himself defended as 'great, hefty howl-verse, as strong and meaty as that other of mine was lovely and be-winged':

Noel! Noel! Noel! Noel!
A Catholic tale have I to tell!
And a Christian song have I to sing
While all the bells in Arundel ring.

(For full version see p. 134)

Out on the main road, the A285, I walked north and, after about half a mile, came to the Cricketers' Arms with its brave sign of the redoubtable Dr W.G. Grace at the wicket. In 1950 on Thursday 16 February I stayed overnight. I had arrived at teatime, having walked from Storrington that day, and sat in a back room with Mr Phillips, the landlord, his wife and family and had a meal of two boiled eggs – an unheard of luxury at that time – bread and jam and homemade cake.

That evening there was a darts match in the bar against a team from some neighbouring village, and I found myself in jovial and genial company. There was a huge blazing fire of cordwood logs up to four feet long and the floor consisted of large, rectangular flagstones. After closing time I helped with the cleaning up. We sluiced the floor down with buckets of hot water and soda and scrubbed it with bass brooms as you would a stable floor. Then after we'd had a nightcap at the bar, Mr Phillips heaped up the white wood ash on the hearth with a large pan-shovel until it completely covered the burning logs in a conical pile, and we left it sending up a lazy spiral of smoke from its apex, like Etna smouldering on a sultry afternoon, and went to bed. But that was long ago.

I reached the door and went in, and there were several people in the bar. It was the sort of pub interior that one has come to expect in these days since inns have been emasculated, so I was not surprised – just disappointed – that those splendid flagstones had been boarded over and covered with a fitted carpet. At least the inglenook fireplace was still there, albeit with logs of more modest proportions, a large fire having been rendered unnecessary by central heating.

On the wall was a photograph of a crowd of villagers assembled outside the inn on the occasion of Edward VII's coronation, which had warranted the turning out of the local brass band. It is dated 1902, the year of the original walk. The landlord told me that the inn was at one time owned by the Deane family, who are to be seen in another picture, seated in front of the old fireplace. James Deane was a celebrated cricketer and used to walk from Duncton to play for Sussex at Brighton. At that time it was known as the Swan Inn, but in 1860 John Wisden took it over and changed the name to the Cricketers' Arms.

It was outside this inn where Myself had said:

Very well then, let us go into the Cricketers' Arms, where Mr Justice Honeybubble went when I was a boy, and there delivered his famous Opinion: his Considered Opinion, his Opinion of permanent value, his Opinion which is the glory of the law.

Inside this same bar, in front of this very fireplace, he had told the tale of how Mr Justice Thingumbob Honeybubble had 'harangued the men of Duncton' and delivered his celebrated summing-up of the dispute between 'George and Roland', the matter of which was 'Two pigs, "Maaster", Mas'r Burt, the change of a sovereign and Chichester market'. This had left the peasants in the bar, and even the disputants themselves, more bewildered about the complexities of the law than they had been about the dispute in the first place. Once again I counted myself lucky to have known the Cricketers' Arms before it had been updated, and to remember it much as it must have been when Belloc told the tale.

Later I walked up the road to the Old Post Office where I had booked in for the night.

Duncton to South Harting (13 miles)

Soon after nine the next morning I set off again to the intense excitement of a
humorous golden Labrador pup belonging to the household, who kept darting
about in all directions, jumping up and barking with his tail wagging furiously, all
the while wearing a facial expression remarkably like a human smile. It was a
pleasant send off and, having decided not to follow the road to the north, which
leads round to Graffham, as my predecessors probably had, I took the public
footpath westward, which runs up by the side of the Old Post Office, and across
the fields to Ridlington Farm, Westerlands Stud and Lower Barn. Keeping to the
north of Upper Norwood I would eventually come out onto the road just to the
north-east of Graffham.

The lands were very well farmed and ploughing had begun on the wide open
fields. Here and there the freshly turned earth showed through the stubbles in
strips, like a brown cord waistcoat worn under a tweed jacket, and at Lower Barn

Graffham, a village under the Downs

the Dutch barns were stacked solid to the roofs with bales of sweet-smelling hay. Due south from here is Littleton Down, which at 253 metres is the highest point in the whole range of the South Downs.

When Belloc and his company left the Cricketers' Arms at Duncton they had strung out along the road with Grizzlebeard taking the lead, followed by the Poet, and the Sailor and Myself bringing up the rear. They had all agreed to meet at the 'next inn whatever it might be', and in due course the rearguard came across the Poet waiting outside an inn at Graffham.

So we turned into that little house as in duty bound, seeing that it was five miles since we had last acknowledged the goodness of God in the drinking of ale, which is a kind of prayer, as it says in the motto:
Laborare est orare sed potare clarior,
which signifies that work is noble, and prayer its equal, but that drinking good ale is a more renowned and glorious act than any other to which man can lend himself . . .
But when we came to the house, and turned into it, we found that Grizzlebeard, who had gone in already before us, was in that short time deeply engaged with a Stranger who, maugre Heaven, was drinking tea!
There they sat, hardly noticing our entry, and were at it hammer and tongs in an argument.
The Stranger was a measly sort of fellow in a cloak, tall, and with a high voice and words of a cultured kind, and his eyes were like dead oysters, which are unpleasing things; and he and Grizzlebeard, though they had so recently met, were already in the midst of as terrible a balderdash of argument as ever the good angels have permitted on this sad earth.

The argument was on a high philosophical plane, and so completely immersed in discussion were the two of them that his friends left Grizzlebeard to it and adjourned to the public bar:

The Sailor (to the Poet and Myself). Let us go hence, my children, and drink in the bar with common men, for the Devil will very soon come in by the window and fly away with these philosophers. Let us be apart in some safe place when the struggle begins.

After about twenty minutes they returned to find Grizzlebeard and the Stranger still locked in verbal combat with greater passion than ever:

The Sailor (in a solemn tone). Grizzlebeard! Darkness will soon fall upon the Weald, and before it falls we must be beyond Graffham, nay, far beyond. So make up your mind, either to differ with this honest gentleman, or to give way to him here and at once. And in any case you are to find your God (and here he took out his watch) within exactly ten minutes from now, for if you do not we will find Him for you in a sudden way. So in ten minutes find us also in the common bar, or perish in your sins!

Then they left them again, but, as after the allotted time there was still no sign of

Grizzlebeard, they went back once more only to find the argument still proceeding in full flood, the disputants like 'two dogs wrangling in the street'. But on the second visit the Sailor took with him a full tankard of beer.

Then he went in ahead of us, and we all came in behind, and when we came in neither Grizzlebeard nor the Stranger looked up for one moment, but Grizzlebeard was saying, with vast scorn:
    You are simply denying cause and effect, or rather efficient causality.'
    To which the Stranger answered solemnly, 'I do!'
    On hearing this reply the Sailor, very quickly and suddenly, hurled over him all that was in the pint pot of beer, saying hurriedly as he did so, 'I baptize you in the name of the five senses,' and having done so, ran out as hard as he could with us two at his heels, and pegged it up the road at top speed, and never drew rein until he got to the edge of Jockey's Spinney half a mile away, and we following, and running hard close after, and there we found him out of breath and laughing, gasping and catching, and glorying in his great deed.

The next inn *I* came to was The Foresters at Graffham, and I am firmly convinced that this is where this extraordinary event took place. I went in, ordered a drink and sat down to turn again to *the book*. Derek, the landlord, was a personable young man and showed a great deal of interest in the fact that his inn features in a book of such distinction. Together we read the passages referring to the inn and, although now the whole of the ground floor has been opened out into one room, including some of the previously domestic quarters, it is quite obvious that there were at one time two rooms open to the public – a small parlour and a larger public bar – divided by a chimney-piece. In the larger room is a huge inglenook fireplace with a large, ornate fireback, a splendid pair of firedogs and hung about with several iron artefacts of days gone by. It is easy to imagine that this is the bar to which the Sailor, the Poet and Myself adjourned while their friend was so deeply engaged in philosophical debate in the smaller room on the other side of the fireplace.

Out on the road westward past the White Horse Inn, at a point where the road turns abruptly to the north toward Fair Acres and Adams' Farm, I turned south-west on to a private concrete road, open to pedestrians. This leads to Woodcote Farm and on to Hayland's Farm. Just before reaching Hayland's I turned right over a stile with a white-painted top rail on to a public footpath with a fingerpost.

Here the Downs are seen at their most majestic. Their steep, thickly wooded slopes, in all their green burgeoning glory, taper towards the west in a diminishing line: all along from Heyshott Down, Bepton Down, Linch Down, Didling Hill and Treyford Hill, to Beacon Hill surmounted by an aerial mast south of Elsted, until they cross the county border. And away to the north-west in the far distance is the range of hills that belong to Hampshire.

Beech Barn sat in a wide expanse of newly ploughed land and was rather tumbledown, its tiled roof and tarred weatherboarded sides sadly in need of attention, yet still serviceable. I walked up through Manor Farm where I turned left on to a well-metalled track, which led me down until I came to New Barn and, a little farther on, Sunwool Farm. The track is banked on either side with high hazel hedges, and the surrounding fields were crawling with pheasants, which took no notice of my passing.

By the side of a small cottage at Sunwool Farm a tiny stream of limpid water ran freely down from out of the chalk hills, which rear mightily a short distance to the south. Bright green tresses of river crowsfoot waved in the current like a maiden's hair in the breeze, while the yellow, globular blossoms on clumps of monkey flower (*Mimulus guttatus*) danced on their stems in the eddying shallows at the edges.

I came up past Cocking Church out onto the A286 at about noon, and there right opposite was the Potter and Vine Inn, which, when I first went in there in 1950, was called The Bluebell. We know that Belloc called here, and this will be made clear a litte later on.

After a lunch of bread, cheese and bitter I set out again along Bell Lane, soon passing a cottage on the south side of the road built of chalk blocks with brick quoins. This material is used widely in these parts for cottages and farm buildings. I looked at the walls closely and found that the chalk was of a very much harder variety than that which is found in the chalk cliffs on the coast in my own part of the county; in fact it is more like limestone. It is cut into square blocks so that the grain runs diagonally from corner to corner. In building a wall, care must be taken to ensure that the grain runs from a high point on the interior surface to a low one on the exterior, so that condensation and other moisure will seep through the block from the inside down to the outside and not the reverse.

I passed the bottom of Bepton Street and soon after, just to the west of the venerable old Rectory, I came to the church with its short, square tower and Sussex cap almost hidden in the trees. On I went past Linch Farm and into Bugshill Lane, always with the rolling wave of the Downs away to my left. Treyford Hill is one of the heights here not clothed with foliage and its precipitous northern face was dotted with sheep clinging to the grassy slopes like mountain goats.

We have already talked about the many points of contact on this walk that coincide at least favourably, and sometimes identically, with locations mentioned in *the book*, but there is one notable failure. I did not on either of the two walks ever find anything that remotely resembles the inn where the Four Men feasted and in which they spent the last night of their journey.

The Old Road

When they were 'but a mile or two from the County border' they debated a feast that should mark the completion of the walk and the parting of their ways:

'My friends,' said I, 'all men before death make a feast if they can. . . .

. . . Now, with to-morrow morning we shall come to the end of this little journey of ours, all along the County, all the way from end to end. Thus we shall attain, as you may say, the death of our good time. For it is agreed between us that when we come to the Hampshire border we shall separate and see each other no more.'

That they should have a feast was agreed by all, and when they were discussing who should pay for it the Poet assured them that he had nothing left. Myself enquired:

'How is this, Poet? It was only to-day that I saw you with my own eyes at the Bluebell paying for a mug of beer with a labouring man.'

The Poet. 'It was my last money, and I did it for charity.'
The Sailor. 'Then now you may have the reward of charity and starve.'

So here is our first pointer. They had already been to The Bluebell and so, by necessity, must be on the west side of Cocking. Then:

As we thus decided upon the nature of the feast, the last of the light, long declined, had faded upon the horizon behind the lattice-work of bare branches. The air was pure and cold, as befitted All-Hallows, and the far edges of the Downs toward the Hampshire border had level lines of light above them, deeply coloured, full of departure and of rest. There was a little mist upon the meadows of the Rother, and a white line of it in the glowing darkness under the edges of the hills. It was not yet quite dark, but the first stars had come into the sky, and the pleasant scent of the wood fires was already strong upon the evening air when we found ourselves outside a large inn standing to the north of the road, behind a sort of green recess or common. Here were several carts standing out in the open, and a man stood with a wagon and a landaulette or two, and dogcarts as well, drawn up in the great courtyard.
    The lower rooms of this old inn were brilliantly lighted. The small square panes of it were shaded with red curtains, through which that light came to us on our cold evening way, and we heard the songs of men within; for there had been some sort of sale, I think, which had drawn to this place many of the farmers from around, and some of the dealers and other smaller men.

They entered and feasted on eggs and bacon with cheese and cottage loaves. Then, contented and filled, they lit their pipes and sipped their individual choices of drink: blackcurrant port, brandy, beer and claret. Then, with the assembled company of fifteen to twenty men, they joined in an evening of song. This is where the old man struck the board loudly with his fist and cried, 'Golier', at which the rest broke out in chorus:

When this verse (which is the whole of the poem) had been repeated some six times, I knew myself indeed to be still in my own County, and I was glad inside my heart, like a man who hears the storm upon the windows, but is himself safe houseled by the fire. So did I know Hampshire to be stretching waste a mile or two beyond, but here was I safe among my own people by the token that they were singing that ancient song 'Golier'.

Belloc's account of that evening reflects how thoroughly he enjoyed an occasion of this nature and contrasts sharply with Beckett's rather soured view of the men singing in the bar at Sutton.
    The inn was full to capacity and some had to sleep on straw in the barn, but our travellers were given blankets and rugs and they slept 'the last sleep of that good journeying' on the floor in front of the bar room fire.
    The next morning they were up and on the road again at first light, and here we get another clue: 'For a mile and a second mile and a third no one of us spoke a word to another'.
    And then they came to Treyford. So the inn must have been about three miles

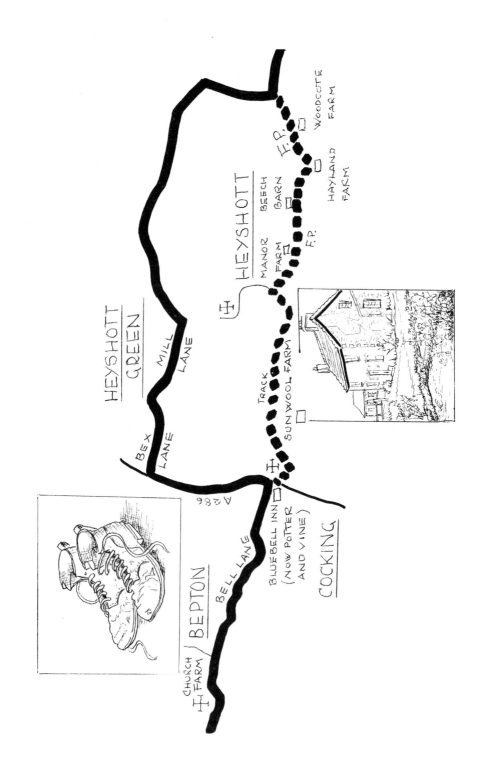

HEYSHOTT GREEN

MILL LANE

BEX LANE

HEYSHOTT

MANOR FARM

BEECH BARN

F.P.

F.P.

WOODCOTE FARM

HAYLAND FARM

TRACK

SUNWOOL FARM

A286

BLUEBELL INN
(NOW POTTER AND VINE)

COCKING

BELL LANE

CHURCH FARM / BEPTON

east of Treyford and somewhere west of Cocking. Though I looked diligently I was unable to find a house that might once have been an inn, or any other building or even a ruin that would fit into the jigsaw and complete the picture. It must, therefore, if indeed it ever existed, remain a mystery, at least for the time being.

Heavy storm clouds were curdling and building up over the wall of the Downs to the south-west, and the wind had freshened as I passed Didling. I left the road and took to the track that leads to Didling Church, which stands quite alone in the fields at the foot of Didling Hill.

In the churchyard to the left of the path, just inside the gate, stands an ancient yew tree, which in 1945 nearly fell victim to the tree-feller's axe. Instructions from the vicar for some of its branches to be lopped had somehow become misinterpreted into a request for the tree to be felled, so the men duly arrived to carry out the job. They made a start with axe and saw, but a timely visit by an observant parishioner caused the work to be halted and the instructions to be checked. The felling was at once called off and the tree was spared. The marks of the axe are still clearly visible at the base of the trunk.

I sat on a seat in the dark green rather sombre shade and stretched my legs for a while. I wondered whether there is any truth in the legend that the church authorities disliked the idea of horses and cattle straying in from the common land and grazing among the tombstones. Being reluctant to go to the expense themselves of building walls to keep the intruders out, they planted yew trees in the graveyards, the berries of which are highly toxic, so that the villagers would build walls to prevent their livestock from going in.

A storm was now imminent, the sky was black and threatening, and rain began to fall in large drops, so I went inside. Dedicated to St Andrew, the church is tiny – a mere 46 feet in length – and unpretentious in the extreme. It was rebuilt on the site of a Saxon church in 1220, a rectangular building with a nave and chancel under one continuous roof with a simple bell-cote at the western end. The plain, white-washed walls and tiled floor carry simplicity almost to the point of austerity, yet manage to retain an atmosphere of warmth and welcome. Much of this, one feels, must arise from the long continuity over the centuries of bringing together so many generations of people to worship.

Most of the windows are single lancets, which have admitted the light of day since the thirteenth century. The sturdy, medieval oak benches are still in use, although backs were added in the eighteenth century and the worn and worm-eaten seats were relined some years later. The old bench-ends are fitted with iron candle-holders, and even to this day on dark winter evenings services are conducted and followed in the psalters and prayer books by candlelight. Here in this humble house of God, over all those centuries, country folk of the locality have knelt to praise the Lord who made the hills, sending up their prayers of supplication and singing their hymns of joy and adulation.

From a pamphlet I learned that it is known as The Shepherds' Church, probably because the shepherds who tended their flocks on the Downs used it as a place of worship. One can imagine that, in their smocks and heavy boots, they would have felt more comfortable here than in perhaps a cathedral or a church of a higher order. A certain amount of theatre, of course, is necessary in the church's approach to its people, but too much pomp and pageantry can have an adverse effect.

Didling is certainly my kind of church. A plain service in a church like this with unaccompanied hymns sung by candlelight in ancient oak pews, with straightforward talk from the pulpit, a hand-embroidered altar cloth and laneside flowers gathered by village children, offers far more to me than the spectacle and ceremony of the higher church orders with their mitres, croziers and incense.

The storm had moved right in under the hill by this time and the daylight was all but gone. Flashes of lightning repeatedly lit the interior of the church, followed by angry cannonades of thunder. I was standing by the Saxon font, which was hewn in solid stone taken from the Bracklesham Beds on the coast, about a dozen miles away, when there was a terrifying flash of electric-blue lightning. Immediately the heavens overhead split asunder with a terrific crack of thunder, which went rolling and rumbling away over the hills like the clatter of buffers in a shunting yard.

I went to the door and was standing just inside the porch looking out, when suddenly the rain ceased. All was quiet again save the drip, drip of rain from the yew tree and the dribbling from over-flowing gutters. The sun peeped through and gleamed on the path and the long cross embossed on an ancient iron-stone tomb lying flat in the long drenched grasses. As I passed through the gate and out onto the track again I fancied I could hear faint chanting and the rolling Latin phrases from some Franciscan plainsong rising up behind me. Were the ghosts of over seven hundred years stirring in their slumber?

Reflecting on St Andrew's alias of The Shepherds' Church brought to mind the old Sussex custom for shepherds to be buried with a lock of wool on their chests. This explained that their absences from church on Sundays had been the result of their tending their flocks, thus excusing them. I wrote the following poem:

A Shepherd's Prayer

On a summer Sunday evening
For a brief half hour of ease,
Ben, the shepherd, sits and ponders
While the sun shines through the trees,
And the honey bees buzz softly
As they blunder to and fro'
From the purple-spotted foxgloves
To the white hives in a row.

Here his garden is untended
And the nettles grow waist high;
In the ash tree zephyrs whisper
Softer than a maiden's sigh.
Down the path he looks with pleasure
At the runner beans grown tall,
And the ripen-ing tomatoes
Up against the churchyard wall.

Sees the rows of peas and carrots
And the rosemary and sage,

All laid out with neat precision
Like the printing on a page.
Sees he, too, the jackdaw perching
On the steeple weather-vane.
Hears the laughter of the children
Playing hop-scotch down the lane.

Now the week has turned full circle
And the wheels have ceased to spin,
Opens he his heart to heaven
And lets peace come drifting in.
All is well and life is moving
On its due appointed course
Following in blind obedience
To some hallowed, unknown force.

CLANG! The bells crash from the belfry
And his thoughts are all undone,
Flying like a flock of starlings

When they hear the keeper's gun.
Then from cottage, hall or farm or
Other places where they dwell,
Come the faithful, trotting briskly
To the summons of the bell.

Meeting at the ancient lych-gate,
Greeting with a nod and smile,
On their Sunday-best behaviour,
Dressed in best but sober style.
Clutching in their hands their prayer-
   books,
Hurrying e'er the hymn begins.
Clutching, also, in their hearts
Their little weekly crop of sins.

Grocermen who give short measure
Mixing sugar up with sand,
Men who climb another's staircase
While he's working on the land.
Practicers of greed and gossip
Here for absolution seek
To emerge, the service over,
Blameless for another week.

Some attend from merely habit,
Some are on the Church guild list,
Others only make appearance
Lest their presence might be missed.

In the church 'twas dark and gloomy
And the air was dank and chill.
Outside in a blaze of fire the
Sun went down behind the hill.
Ben gazed up in silent wonder
At the green gold afterglow,
Watched with awe a single star
Shed twinkling light on earth below.

'I en't, Lord, had no truck with church –
Shepherds dun't have time t' go.
They used t' put a lock o' wool
Inside their coffins so You'd know.
I likes t' watch the sky be night
An' see how bright that star do shine,
But, if church be the only road to
   Heaven,
Here's one, O Lord, as wun't be
   gwine.'

A little less than a mile further on I came to Treyford where one of the most picturesque roadsigns in the county is to be found. It is a beautifully carved figure of St Christopher with the haloed Christ child on his shoulder. His left hand points northwards toward Harting and he is holding a staff in his right hand. The figures are tastefully coloured and the whole is mounted on a sturdy oak post with a wooden canopy to keep off the worst of the elements. Underneath on the plinth on which the figures are supported is the text: 'Who carried Christ speed thee today, And lift thy heart up all the way.'

I first saw this when I did the walk in 1950, but some time later it mysteriously disappeared and was lamented by all who had known it. A great many years later, just as mysteriously, it reappeared in its original position, refurbished and newly painted with only one small detail impaired. The staff in St Christopher's right hand originally extended up above the hand and bore a pennant that pointed at a right angle to his left hand, directly down the road to the east, and read 'To Cocking'. It is said that this unique waymark had been stolen and the perpetrator of this shameful crime, overcome by pangs of conscience, eventually relented and sought to expiate his sin by returning it to the site from which he had so ignobly removed it. If this is true I think his redemption should be given earnest consideration.

If Didling possesses one of the most appealing of all the many 'little, lost Downland churches' in Sussex, then Treyford, its next-door neighbour, possesses

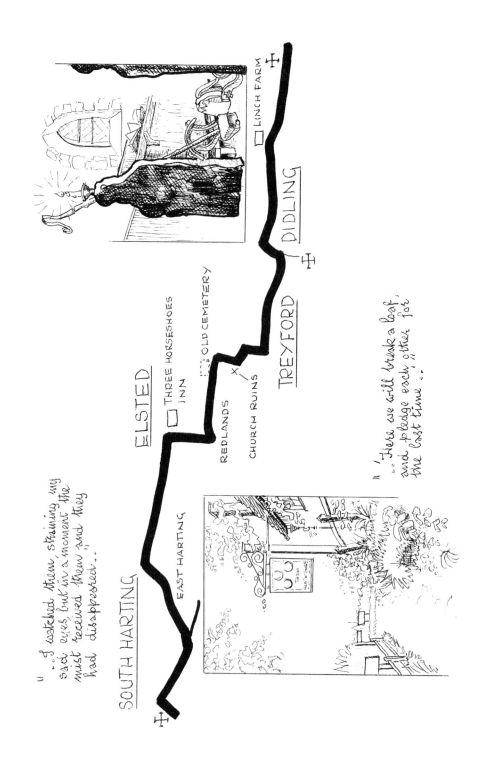

SOUTH HARTING

EAST HARTING

"... I watched them straining my sad eyes, but in a moment the mist received them and they had disappeared ..."

ELSTED

☐ THREE HORSESHOES INN

REDLANDS

🏛 OLD CEMETERY

X
CHURCH RUINS

TREYFORD

DIDLING

☐ LINCH FARM

"... Here we will break a loaf, and pledge each other for the last time ..."

none at all. But that this is the result of apathy or lack of godliness is repudiated by the fact that the village has the remains of two. The earlier one, which was in the street itself, fell into disrepair and disuse about a hundred and fifty years ago. It had been dedicated to St Mary and many of the tombs in the churchyard were of the Aylwin family, which dates back in the area to the sixteenth century. But we read in Arthur Beckett's 'The Spirit of the Downs' how the tiles were taken to roof the school of a neighbouring village and that the 'weathers' had completed what man had thus begun. The sad pile of ivy-creepered walls and overgrown rubble remain to this day.

Picturesque road sign, Treyford

The church that replaced it, St Peter's, was built on the hill just outside the village and was consecrated in 1849, having been erected through the generosity of Lady Harcourt. The spire was 120 feet high and, already being on an eminence, was a conspicuous landmark for miles around. In my notes on the 1950 walk I wrote, 'Along past Bepton Church with its squat, square tower standing on a little mound of green pastureland, I followed the road under Linch Down with the busy sound of the circular saw quivering across the clear afternoon air from Linch Farm and the slender, pointed spire of Treyford Church always ahead.'

The traveller along this road today will be denied that sight, for once again the local house of prayer was allowed to disintegrate. One story has it that much of the steeple was built of local chalk, and the cardinal rule regarding the laying of blocks so that the moisture gravitates toward the outside of the building and not the inside, as outlined above, was disregarded. Thus the building became unsafe and had to be demolished some time in the late 1950s. Today there is not one stone on top of another, but the outline of its foundations, apparent in the debilitated nature and different colour of the grass, is clearly defined. To the south of this are the stones and wooden crosses that mark the graves of earlier parishioners. Some overgrown with brambles stand deserted and rather desolate here on the hill just outside the village, but all affections and remembrances are not dead, and one is heartened by the one or two graves bearing vases of fresh cut flowers that tell of continuing devotions.

As I went on toward Redlands I wondered if there might be any mysterious connection between the sad demise of two churches in one village and the fact that, no more than a mile away over the brow of Treyford Hill, a line of five conical barrows, some nearly 20 feet high, are known as The Devil's Jumps. At least *his* edifices in this area would appear to be the more durable.

At Redlands a sharp right-hand turn led me up into the village of Elsted, where at the top of the hill another right turn took me in a short time to the Three Horse Shoes Inn standing high up on the rocks at the side of the lane. The garden of the inn was an excellent vantage point from which to look back over the lovely country I had walked through during the day, with the long chain of hills behind.

When we had come to Treyford, Grizzlebeard, who was by dumb assent at this moment our leader, or at any rate certainly mine, took that lane northward which turns through Redlands and up to the hill of Elstead and its inn. Then for the first time he spoke and said:

Elstead (Elsted), where at the inn the Four Men broke a loaf and pledged each other for the last time

'Here we will break a loaf, and pledge each other for the last time.'
Which we did, all sitting quite silent.

It was by this time early evening and the inn was open. On the path just outside the door were five pairs of slightly muddy walking boots placed neatly side by side. I lifted the old iron lift-latch on the door and entered, and there in the bar seated on a long settle were five ladies in their stockinged feet, sitting in as neat a line as were their boots on the bricks outside. We nodded and smiled the kind of non-committal greetings that fellow walkers exchange, but as I had been walking on the hard high road and my boots were clean, it was not necessary for me to join them in performing the ritual of removing my footwear before entering. The brick floor of the bar was uneven and worn down by the hob-nails and iron pelts of the boots of labouring men, whose bar it was in the days before such niceties were observed.

I went into a small room to the left of the main bar, which itself was not large, and ordered a pint of locally brewed Sussex bitter through the hatch. Immediately I felt an overwhelming conviction that this was the room in which the Four Men unceremoniously broke a loaf and pledged each other for the last time. It was in surroundings like these that Belloc found himself most at home and in tune with life. No one could have been more in love with the countryside inns of England. The room remains unchanged: the friendly fireplace, the simple seating around the walls; plain, serviceable and hospitable. Here they sat in a pregnant silence knowing that they were soon to part for ever.

I, too, sat in silence thinking of his songs, his poems and his undying prose, and my mind was alive with the Bellocian legacy and everything it stands for: the Sussex countryside and Sussex folk; places like this; ale like this; good company; good songs and worthwhile talk – in short, the warm companionship of good Sussex inns. I learned from the landlord that Mrs Tullett, who was born at the inn and whose parents were the inn-keepers, was still alive in a cottage close by. In 1902 when Belloc called she would have been in her cradle.

The road out of the village westward has no footpath, but the grass verges are flat and I had no problem with passing traffic. Two miles further on I came to South Harting and the goal to which I had been striding for the past six days.

> . . . and then again we took the road, and went forward as we had gone forward before, until we came to Harting.

Just before they had reached Treyford Belloc had dropped a hint that his fellow travellers were not quite as other men:

> But as I walked along I looked furtively first to one side and then to the other, judging my companions, whom chance had given me for these few hours; and it seemed to me (whether from the mist or what not) that they were taller than men; and their eyes avoided my eyes.

I stood there under the sign of the Ship Inn looking down the deserted street flanked by the creeper-covered walls and crooked gables of centuries-old houses, which had been the setting for that poignant farewell scene between Myself and his companions. I took *the book* from my pocket and read:

> And when we came to Harting, just in the village street of it, Grizzlebeard, going forward a little more quickly, drew with him his two companions, and they stood before me, barring the road as it were, and looking at me kindly, but halting my advance.

The Street, South Harting, 'Then they all three turned about and went rapidly and with a purpose up the village street'

I said to them, a little afraid, 'Do you make for our parting now? We are not yet come to the county border!'

But Grizzlebeard said (the others keeping silent): 'Yes. As we met upon this side of the county border, so shall we part before we cross it. Nor shall you cross it with us. But these my companions and I, when we have crossed it must go each to our own place: but you are perhaps more fortunate, for you are not far from your own home.'

When he had said this, I was confused to wonder from his voice and from the larger aspect of himself and his companions, whether indeed they were men.

'Come back with me,' I said, 'along the crest of the Downs; we will overlook together the groves at Lavington and the steep at Bury Combe, and then we will turn south and reach a house I know upon the shingle, upon the tide, near where the Roman palaces are drowned beneath the Owers; and to-night once more, and if you will for the last time, by another fire we will sing yet louder songs, and mix them with the sound of the sea.'

But Grizzlebeard would not even linger. He looked at me with a dreadful solemnity and said: 'No; we are all three called to other things. But do you go back to your home, for the journey is done.'

. . . the other two, looking sadly at me, stood silent also for about the time in which a man can say good-bye with reverence. Then they all three turned about and went rapidly and with a purpose up the village street.

I watched them, straining my sad eyes, but in a moment the mist received them and they had disappeared.

At the far end of the street, like a shrine, the green, copper-sheathed steeple of the church was framed in the trees. I closed the pages. My pilgrimage was complete.

Epilogue

I was met and driven home by car. In the garden I paused and looked southward. The night was fine and warm. Stars over the sea were winking down at the lights of the inshore trawlers working the fishing grounds, and Jupiter was still there bright and sparkling as ever, peeping through a gap in the ash tree.

I went indoors and my two cats came to greet me, weaving round my ankles with perpendicular tails and purring like sewing machines. The brass-dialled grandfather clock in the corner of the room was still ticking the seconds away one by one, and the comforting arms of hearth and home wrapped warmly about me.

During the many hours of walking alone in the open country in all weathers I had become more aware of the surrounding moods of nature and felt on closer terms with my native county. The eternity of the earth and sky, the beauty of the autumnal countryside and all the warmth of good fellowship had combined to make the journey a rewarding experience.

Sussex has changed, of course, but it has changed far less than might be imagined by anyone not looking closely enough. I had discovered that the true Sussex still lives, and speaks with a thousand voices, and even sings for those that have ears to hear. I had returned with a greater understanding of the deep, unchanging influences of thought and feeling that have gone into building the character of its villages and its people. There is an affinity with the past – a common thread of continuity that links the present day with years gone by and tethers a Sussex man to his native soil. I had heard the voices of the days of long ago and they struck a deep chord of recognition in my heart:

> They told of lonely, all-night vigil in the lambing-pen,
> And long hard days of sweat at haying-time;
> Of evening walks along the bridle path
> With long, lingering pauses at the kissing-gate,
> An unseen cuckoo calling repeatedly
> In answer to the echo
> Of its own wood-wind notes across the vale;
> Of gathering cowslips on the steep green slopes
> In early summer, and searching the autumn dews
> For pink-finned mushrooms;
> Of fetching the morning milk in frothing cans
> And taking warm, brown eggs from under nesting hens.
>
> So much there was in our young lives that
> Mingled into the patterns of the past

That fact can scarcely be defined
From stories handed down.

The straining horse teams and the lumbering wains
Were part of our lives just as much as theirs.
The same jokes, the same songs,
The same old jobs, the same old tools –
Why, Thomas Tusser's shepherd would have felt at home –
And the strong arms that swung the scythes
In the green fields of summer
Were those that sprung the long bows
At the Battle of Agincourt:
The rough voices that shouted the teams to greater effort
In the shafts of the hay wagons
Had urged to victory the great war-horses at Crecy.

In spite of world-shaking eruptions in the form of war
There prevailed a cosy insularity and self-deluding trust
That things would never change.
Small wonder, then, that sometimes
We cast a wistful eye back over our shoulders
And recall the simple riches that were ours.

Who has stood and watched a crimson dawn come up
In solitary and spine-tingling wonderment;
Or laughed and sung a magic midnight hour
Into another day with roistering friends,
Cannot die a poor man.
Who has felt the stab of death's intrusion
Into the close-knit circle known as home,
But lived to see the fruitful widening of the rings,
Like ripples on the surface of a pond,
And heard the innocent laughter of grandchildren
Soothing away the anguish of the past,
Has riches beyond the grasp of miser's greed.

I have seen little of this world. My light has been
But a tiny tallow-dip in a tythe barn;
But if love, laughter and joy in simple things
Be the golden draught of life,
My God, I have drunk deep.
My cup is getting low –
Pass me the flagon will you, please.

Belloc's Songs

Belloc was a man of diverse abilities. One of the lesser known instruments in his orchestra of talents was an exceedingly good ear for a tune. But in the brilliance of his achievements as poet, novelist, historian, economist and artist – to name but a few of his various pursuits – this humbler gift of creating tuneful melodies tends to pass unnoticed.

Though not a musician in the technical sense, he had a natural flare for the tuneful. Songs and singing were an essential part of his life and scarcely a day went by without a little assistance from his pleasantly musical tenor voice. Music hall ditties, red-nosed comic choruses or marching songs from his service days in the French cavalry would all come spilling out from time to time, revealing his susceptibility to a pleasing refrain.

He set some of his poems, and sometimes the poems of others, to his own tunes. But he lacked the necessary skills to put them down on paper and, were it not for his cousin, Dorothy Swainson, an accomplished musician in her own right, who transformed several of his songs into musical notation, an important facet of this remarkable man would have been lost to us. This is a selection of his songs, which illustrate the range of moods of which he was capable and his skill in composing a tune eminently suitable to the subject of a poem.

I could find no record of Belloc having composed tunes to the 'West Sussex Drinking Song' and 'Duke William' so have adapted traditional Sussex tunes to his words.

On Sussex Hills

On Sussex hills where I was bred,
When lanes in autumn rains are red,
When Arun tumbles in his bed,
And busy great gusts go by;
When branch is bare in Burton Glen
And Bury Hill is a-whitening, then,
I drink strong ale with gentlemen;
Which nobody can deny, deny,
Deny, deny, deny, deny,
Which nobody can deny!

In half-November off I go,
To push my face against the snow,
And watch the winds wherever they blow,
Because my heart is high:
Till I settle me down in Steyning to sing
Of the women I met in my wandering,

And of all that I mean to do in the spring.
Which nobody can deny, deny,
Deny, deny, deny, deny,
Which nobody can deny!

Then times be rude and weather be rough,
And ways be foul and fortune tough,
We are of the stout South Country stuff,
That never can have good ale enough,
And do this chorus cry!
From Crowboro' Top to Ditchling Down,
From Hurstpierpoint to Arundel town,
The girls are plump and the ale is brown:
Which nobody can deny, deny,
Deny, deny, deny, deny,
If he does he tells a lie!

The Pelagian Heresy

Pelagius lived in Kardanoel,
And taught a doctrine there,
How whether you went to Heaven or Hell,
It was your own affair.
How, whether you found eternal joy
Or sank for ever to burn,
It had nothing to do with the Church, my boy,
But was your own concern.

Oh, he didn't believe
In Adam and Eve,
He put no faith therein!
His doubts began
With the fall of man,
And he laughed at original sin!

With my row-ti-tow, ti-oodly-ow,
He laughed at original sin!

Whereat the Bishop of old Auxerre
(Germanus was his name),
He tore great handfuls out of his hair,
And he called Pelagius Shame:
And then with his stout Episcopal staff
So thoroughly thwacked and banged
The heretics all, both short and tall,
They rather had been hanged.

  Oh, he thwacked them hard, and he banged them long,
  Upon each and all occasions,
  Till they bellowed in chorus, loud and strong,
  Their orthodox persuasions!

  With my row-ti-tow, ti-oodly-ow,
  Their orthodox persua-a-a-sions!

Now the Faith is old and the Devil is bold,
Exceedingly bold indeed;
And the masses of doubt that are floating about
Would smother a mortal creed.
But we that sit in a sturdy youth,
And still can drink strong ale,
Oh – let us put it away to infallible truth,
Which always shall prevail!

  And thank the Lord
  For the temporal sword,
  And howling heretics too;
  And whatever good things
  Our Christendom brings,
  But especially barley brew!

  With my row-ti-tow, ti-oodly-ow,
  Especially barley brew!

His Hide is Covered with Hair

The dog is a faithful, intelligent friend,
But his hide is covered with hair;
The cat will inhabit the house to the end,
But *her* hide is covered with hair.

The hide of the mammoth was covered with wool,
The hide of the porpoise is sleek and cool,
But you'll find, if you look at that gambolling fool,
That his hide is covered with hair.

Chorus
   Oh, I thank my God for this at the least,
   I was born in the West and not in the East,
   And He made me a human instead of a beast,
   Whose hide is covered with hair!

The cow in the pasture that chews the cud,
Her hide is covered with hair,
And even a horse of the Barbary blood,
His hide is covered with hair.

The camel excels in a number of ways,
And travellers give him unlimited praise –
He can go without drinking for several days –
But his hide is covered with hair.

Chorus

The bear of the forest that lives in a pit,
His hide is covered with hair;
The laughing hyena in spite of his wit,
His hide is covered with hair!

The Barbary ape and the chimpanzee,
And the lion of Africa, verily he,
With his head like a wig, and the tuft on his knee,
His hide is covered with hair.

Chorus

The Delicate Flower

When I was not much older
Than Cupid, but bolder,
I asked of his Mother in passing her bower
What it was in their blindness
Men asked of her kindness,
And she said it was naught but a delicate flower,
Oh a delicate, delicate, delicate flower!

This morning you kissed me,
By noon you dismissed me
As though such great things were the jest of one hour,
And you left me still wondering
If I were not too blundering
To deal with that delicate, delicate flower:
'Tis such a delicate, delicate, delicate flower!

For if that's the complexion
Of Ladies' affection
I must needs be a fool to remain in their power;
But there's that in me burning
Which brings me returning
To beg for the delicate, delicate flower;
To implore for that delicate, delicate flower!

West Sussex Drinking Song

They sell good beer at Haslemere
And under Guildford Hill.
At Little Cowfold as I've been told
A beggar may drink his fill:
There is a good brew in Amberley too,
And by the bridge also;
But the swipes they take in at Washington Inn
Is the very best Beer I know.

Chorus
  With my here it goes, and there it goes,
  All the fun's before us:
  The Tipple's aboard and the night is young,
  The door's ajar and the Barrel is sprung,

I am singing the best song ever was sung
  And it has a rousing chorus.

If I were what I never can be,
The master or the squire:
If you gave me the hundred from here to the sea,
Which is more than I desire:
Then all my crops should be barley and hops,
And did my harvest fail
I'd sell every rood of mine acres I would
For a belly-full of good Ale.

Chorus

Duke William

Duke William was a wench's son, his granfer was a tanner! He
drunk his cider from the tun, Which is the Norman manner: His
throne was made of oak and gold, His bow-shaft of the yew —
That is the way the tale is told, I doubt if it be true, I doubt if it be true! But
what care I for him? My tankard is full to the brim, And I'll sing Elizabeth
Dorothy, etc. etc... Pegotty, taut and trim, Pegotty, taut and trim.

Duke William was a wench's son,
His granfer was a tanner!
He drank his cider from the tun,
Which is the Norman manner:
His throne was made of oak and gold,
His bow-shaft of the yew –
That is the way the tale is told,
I doubt if it be true! (Repeat)

But what care I for him?
My tankard is full to the brim,
And I'll sing Elizabeth, Dorothy,
Margaret, Mary, Dorinda,
Persephone, Miriam,
Pegotty, taut and trim. (Repeat)

The men that sailed to Normandy
Foul weather may they find;
For banging about in the waist of a ship
Was never to my mind.
They drink their rum in the glory-hole
In quaking and in fear;
But a better man was left behind,
And he sits drinking beer. (Repeat)

But what care I for the swine?
They never were fellows of mine!
And I'll sing Elizabeth, Dorothy,
Margaret, Mary, Dorinda,
Persephone, Miriam, Pegotty,
Jezebel, Topsy, Andromeda,
Magdalen, Emily, Charity, Agatha,
Beatrice, Anna, Cecilia, Maud,
Cleopatra, Selene, and Jessica . . .
Barbara stout and fine. (Repeat)

The Winged Horse

It's ten years ago today you turned me out o' doors
To cut my feet on flinty lands and stumble down the shores,
And I thought about the all-in-all, oh more than I can tell!
But I caught a horse to ride upon and I rode him very well,
He had flame behind the eyes of him and wings upon his side.
    And I ride, and I ride!

I rode him out of Wantage and I rode him up the hill,
And there I saw the Beacon in the morning standing still,
Inkpen and Hackpen and southward and away
High through the middle airs in the strengthening of the day,
And there I saw the channel-glint and England in her pride.
    And I ride, and I ride!

And once a-top of Lambourne down toward the hill of Clere
I saw the Host of Heaven in rank and Michael with his spear,
And Turpin out of Gascony and Charlemagne the Lord,
And Roland of the marches with his hand upon his sword
For the time he should have need of it, and forty more beside.
    And I ride, and I ride!

For you that took the all-in-all the things you left were three.
A loud voice for singing and keen eyes to see,
And a spouting well of joy within that never yet was dried!
    And I ride.

The Sailor's Carol

Noel! Noel! Noel! Noel!
A Catholic tale have I to tell!
And a Christian song have I to sing
While all the bells in Arundel ring.

I pray good beef and I pray good beer
This holy night of all the year,
But I pray detestable drink for them
That give no honour to Bethlehem.

May all good fellows that here agree
Drink Audit Ale in heaven with me,
And may all my enemies go to hell!
Noel! Noel! Noel! Noel!
May all my enemies go to hell!
Noel! Noel!

On a Winter's Night

On a winter's night long time ago
(The bells ring loud and the bells ring low),
When high howled wind and down fell snow
(Carillon, Carilla).
Saint Joseph he and Nostre Dame,
Riding on an ass, full weary came
From Nazareth into Bethlehem.
   And the small child Jesus smile on you.

And Bethlehem inn they stood before
(The bells ring less and the bells ring more),
The landlord bade them begone from his door
(Carillon, Carilla).
'Poor folk' (says he), 'must lie where they may,
For the Duke of Jewry comes this way,
With all his train on a Christmas Day.'
   And the small child Jesus smile on you.

Poor folk that may my carol hear
(The bells ring single and the bells ring clear),
See! God's one child had hardest cheer!
(Carillon, Carilla).
Men grown hard on a Christmas morn;
The dumb beast by and a babe forlorn.
It was very, very cold when our Lord was born.
   And the small child Jesus smile on you.

Now these were Jews as Jews must be
(The bells ring merry and the bells ring free).
But Christian men in a band are we
(Carillon, Carilla).
Empty we go, and ill bedight,
Singing Noel on a Winter's night.
Give us to sup by the warm firelight,
   And the small child Jesus smile on you.

The Islands

Sing to me of the Islands, O daughter of Cohoolin, sing.
  Sing to me of the West:
Sing to me of the girth loosened and the lax harp string
  And of rest, and of rest.

Beyond the skerries and beyond the outer water
  There lies the land.
Sing to me of the Islands, O daughter of Cohoolin, O High
  King's daughter.
  And of the Overstrand.

I desire to be with Brandan and his companions in the quiet
  places
  And to drink of their Spring.
Sing to me of the Islands and of the Blessed Faces,
  O Daughter of Cohoolin sing!

Ha'nacker Mill

Sally is gone that was so kindly,
Sally is gone from Ha'nacker Hill.
And the Briar grows ever since then so blindly
And ever since then the clapper is still,
And the sweeps have fallen from Ha'nacker Mill.

Ha'nacker Hill is in Desolation:
Ruin a-top and a field unploughed.
And Spirits that call on a fallen nation
Spirits that loved her calling aloud:
Spirits abroad in a windy cloud.

Spirits that call and no one answers;
Ha'nacker's down and England's done.
Wind and Thistle for pipe and dancers
And never a ploughman under the Sun.
Never a ploughman. Never a one.

Places of Interest near the Route of *The Four Men* Walk

Bodiam Castle   Medieval fortress with moat built 1385. Tearoom, shop, museum. Open daily, varying times through year. Ring for details. Tel: 0580 830436.

Battle Abbey   Built for William the Conqueror on spot where King Harold died. Site of Battle of Hastings 1066. Exhibition, audiovisual presentation. Open daily. Tel: 0424 773792.

Buckley's Yesterday's World, Battle   Museum, garden, children's play village, picnic site. Open daily. Tel: 0424 775378.

Horam Manor, Horam   Home of Merrydown Vintage Cider. Guided tours by advance booking. Open Tuesday to Friday. Tel: 0435 812254.

Bateman's, Burwash   Home of Rudyard Kipling 1902–36. Gardens and water-mill. Open April to October daily except Thursday and Friday. Tel: 0435 882302.

St George's Vineyard, Waldron   Vineyard and winery visits, wine tastings, restaurant. Open Easter to October daily, varying times in winter. Tel: 0435 812156.

Barkham Manor Vineyard, Piltdown   Vineyard trail, winery tour, wine tastings. Eighteenth-century Great Barn. Open April to December daily except Monday. Tel: 0825 722103.

Bluebell Railway, Sheffield Park   Vintage steam train trips, museum, buffet, shop. Open June to September daily, otherwise various. Tel: 0825 722370.

Sheffield Park Garden   Extensive gardens and woodland with five lakes, tearoom, shop. Open April to November Tuesday to Saturday. Sun. afternoons only Oct. and Nov. and Bank Hols. Sun. and Mon. Tel: 0825 790231 or 790655.

Priest House, West Hoathly   Early fifteenth-century timber-framed house, antique furnishings. Open March to October daily except Tuesday. Tel: 0342 810479.

Wakehurst Place, Ardingly   Area of outstanding natural beauty known as 'Kew in the Country'. Tudor mansion, antique furnishings, interpretation area, shop. Open daily. Tel: 081 9401171.

Borde Hill Garden, Haywards Heath   Garden and parkland with lake, pool, woodland, lakeside walks, tearoom, picnic area, restaurant. Open April to October weekdays, Sundays in spring. Tel: 0444 450326.

High Beeches Garden, Handcross   Landscaped woodland garden. Guided tours by appointment. Open April to June, September and October. Ring for details. Tel: 0444 400589.

Nyman's Garden, Handcross   Garden with Italian fountain and laurel walk. Picturesque ruins of house overlook lawns. Open March Saturday and Sunday only, April to October daily except Monday and Friday. Tel: 0444 400321.

Leonardslee Gardens, Lower Beeding   Spectacular woodland gardens with wallabies and deer. Café, restaurant. Open April to October daily. Tel: 0403 891212.

Shipley Windmill, Nr. Horsham   Best known working smock mill in West Sussex. Built in 1879 and restored as a memorial to Hilaire Belloc who lived next door. Open varying times. Enquiries to Mrs A.E. Crowther. Tel: 0403 741310.

King's Land, Shipley, Nr Horsham   Hilaire Belloc's home from 1906 until the time of his death in 1953. Rambling old house preserved much as it was with furnishings, pictures and documents practically as Belloc left them. Still occupied by a member of his family. Guided visits can be arranged if adequate written notice is given. Apply to Mr C. Eustace, King's Land, Shipley, Horsham, West Sussex, RH13 8PL.

Woods Mill Countryside Centre, Henfield   Eighteenth-century water-mill, nature reserve, countryside exhibition, aquarium, audiovisual presentation, refreshment kiosk, picnic area. Open April to October daily except Monday and Friday. Tel: 0273 492630.

St Mary's, Bramber   Fifteenth-century house and gardens with historical, literary and musical connections. Open Easter to September afternoons. Tel: 0903 816205.

Parham House, Pulborough   Elizabethan House and gardens, collection of portraits, tapestries and furniture. Open Easter to October afternoons Sunday, Wednesday, Thursday and Bank Holiday Mondays. Tel: 0903 742021.

Pulborough Brooks Nature Reserve, Wigginholt, Pulborough   Barn Visitor Centre, wildlife walks with scenic views, bird-watching hides. Open daily. Tel: 0798 875851.

Chalk Pits Museum, Amberley   Museum of trades and crafts. Blacksmith, potter, printer, boat-builder, wheel-wright, etc. at work. Narrow-gauge railway, vintage bus trips, tearoom, picnic area. Open March to October daily, extra days in season. Ring for details. Tel: 0798 831370.

Arundel Castle   Historic and picturesque Castle in the Arun valley. Seat of dukes of Norfolk and earls of Arundel for over seven hundred years. Restaurant, shop. Open April to October daily except Saturday. Tel: 0903 883136.

Roman Villa, Bignor   Remains of Roman villa with mosaic floors and underfloor heating (hypocaust). Many mosaic portraits of Venus, Medusa, etc. Museum, cafeteria, picnic area. Open March to October daily except Monday. Tel: 07987 259.

Petworth House and Park   Historic country house, large park, pleasure garden. Beautiful furniture, old masters picture gallery, restaurant, shop. Open April to October daily except Monday and Friday. Tel: 0798 43929.

Weald and Downland Open Air Museum, Singleton   Museum of historic buildings rescued from destruction and rebuilt on downland site. Open March to October daily, Christmas and New Year period: Nov. to Feb. Wed. Sat. and Sun. only. Tel: 0243 811348.

Stansted Park   Stately home, large park, arboretum. Elegant family seat of Earl and Countess Bessborough with continental furniture, pictures and eighteenth-century Brussels tapestries. Events in and around house in season. Open afternoons Easter Sunday and Monday, May to September Sunday, Monday and Tuesday. Tel: 0705 412265.

Summary of Route

Ordnance Survey Maps to which Sketch Maps are Related

Public Transport Information

Trains

(Trains serving towns with bus links to villages on the route)

From London	via	To
Charing Cross	Robertsbridge & Battle	Hastings
Victoria	—	Uckfield
Victoria	Haywards Heath	Lewes
Victoria	Three Bridges, Haywards Heath	Brighton/Shoreham, Worthing
Victoria	Three Bridges, Crawley, Horsham, Pulborough, Amberley, Arundel	Littlehampton/Bognor, Chichester
Waterloo	Guildford, Petersfield	Portsmouth

Buses

To	Company	Service No.	Route
Robertsbridge	LR	4 & 5	Hastings*, Battle*, Robertsbridge*, Maidstone*
Heathfield	SCB	728	Brighton*, Lewes*, Uckfield*, Heathfield, Eastbourne*
Ardingly	GF	472	Haywards Heath*, Ardingly, Three Bridges*, Crawley*
Pease Pottage	BB	33	Haywards Heath*, Pease Pottage, Crawley*
Lower Beeding, Crabtree, Cowfold, Henfield.	CW	137	Horsham*, Lower Beeding, Crabtree, Cowfold, Henfield, Brighton*
Steyning	B&H	20	Shoreham*, Steyning
Washington, Storrington	CW	1 & 1A	Worthing*, Washington, Storrington, Pulborough*, Petworth, Midhurst

West Burton, Bignor, Sutton, Duncton	AM	4	Steyning, Washington, Storrington, Pulborough*, West Burton, Duncton, Chichester* (one journey only)
Cocking	CC	260	Bognor*, Chichester*, Cocking, Midhurst, Hazlemere*, Guildford*
South Harting	HS	61	Petersfield*, South Harting, Elsted, Midhurst

* indicates railway station

(The above is only an outline of the bus services available. For times and further information contact bus company or Tourist Information Office.)

Bus Companies

AM	=	Ambassador Buses	(0798 373581)
B&H	=	Brighton & Hove	(0273 821111)
BB	=	Brighton Buses	(0273 674881)
CC	=	Coastline Chichester	(0243 783251)
CW	=	Coastline Worthing	(0903 237661)
GF	=	Gem Fairtax	(0293 527104)
HS	=	Hants & Sussex	(0243 372045)
LR	=	Local Rider	(0273 478007)
SCB	=	South Coast Buses	(0345 518457)

Bibliography

Beckett, Arthur, *The Spirit of the Downs*, Methuen & Co., 1909.

Belloc, Hilaire, *Hills and the Sea*, Methuen & Co., 1906.

Belloc, Hilaire, *The Four Men*, Nelson, 1912.

Belloc, Hilaire, Introduction to *The Footpath Way*, Sidgwick & Jackson, 1911.

Cook, C.F. (ed.), *The Sussex Book of Verse*, Combridges, 1920.

Morton, J.B., *Hilaire Belloc – A Memoir*, Hollis & Carter, 1955.

Thoreau, Henry, *Walden*

Turner, F.M. (ed.), *The Diary of Thomas Turner*, Bodley Head, 1925.

Picture Credits

Index